S0-EMO-884

41 HIKING TRAILS
NORTHWESTERN CALIFORNIA

BY DON & ROBERTA LOWE

The Touchstone Press
P.O. Box 81
Beaverton, Oregon 97075

Other books by Don and Roberta Lowe

35 Hiking Trails, Columbia River Gorge (1981)
62 Hiking Trails, Northern Oregon Cascades (1979)
60 Hiking Trails, Central Oregon Cascades (1978)
50 West Central Colorado Hiking Trails (1976)
80 Northern Colorado Hiking Trails (1974)

Available from your bookstore or supplier,
or from   THE TOUCHSTONE PRESS
          P.O. BOX 81
          BEAVERTON, OR 97075

Maps Courtesy of
U.S. Geological Survey

Copyright © 1981 by
Don and Roberta Lowe

I.S.B.N. 0-911518-62-2

INTRODUCTION

The convoluted jumble of mountain ranges that comprise northwestern California provides an expanse of hiking and backpacking terrain in the state second only to the Sierra Nevada. Whereas the latter has an ambience of grand, sophisticated elegance, the former is, by comparison, rustic and, in many ways, more demanding of the traveler who ventures from the well trod trails. Another contrast is that the routes in northwestern California are considerably less congested. The visitor who has the pleasure of exploring the interiors of these ranges is treated to a scene of glacier-gnawed peaks, verdant meadows, intense blue skies almost uniform in color from horizon to zenith and clear lakes sprawled or tucked at the base of rocky cirques. Although extremely rugged, this backcountry is at the same time personal, enveloping one who traverses its lush valleys, wooded slopes and open ridges rather than extending into vastness away from him. Not that the traveler ever experiences claustrophobia — along most routes there are many highpoints with far-ranging views to remind him that there's plenty more wildness out there. Also somewhat paradoxically, although the majority of the maintained trails that penetrate the mountains are at the most only moderately demanding in their length and elevation gain, the interiors provide obscure routes and terrain challenging enough even for the most experienced hiker.

The first two hikes described in this guide head north from the Seiad Valley into the Siskiyou Mountains. Hikes 3 through 9 are in the heart of the Marble Mountains and No's. 20 through 38 penetrate the Trinity Alps, a sub-range of the Salmon Mountains. No's. 10 through 19 are in the no less mountainous terrain between the Marbles and Trinities. (You could spend a long winter's evening untangling the maze of mountain ranges in this part of California.) The final three trips are near I-5 with No's. 39 and 40 being adjacent to Mt. Shasta (part of the Cascade range, not the mountain systems to the west) and No. 41 is in the fantastic granite rock outcroppings of The Castle Crags south of Dunsmuir. This final hike is in a state park. All the others described in this guide are on land managed by the U.S. Forest Service.

A special charm of the trails in northwestern California is the variation in terrain and vegetation most of them travel through from trailhead to destination. You'll often begin in a forest of pine, oak and maple, travel through at least one lush meadow and deep fir forest before reaching an exquisite timberline setting of grass over which rocks, trees and small plants have been artistically scattered. Wildflowers are abundant with the best garden being along the trail to Deer Creek Pass (No. 32). Wildlife — deer, birds, bear, the works — likewise are plentiful. Seeing bear would be a special treat as they're such furtive animals but the chances of encountering very young fawns are high. You may even cross paths with the big turtle who lives along the Granite Lake Trail (No. 31). The fish population is dense and lakes are noted for good catches.

The only criticism of northwestern California from the hiker's standpoint is that it's uncomfortably hot from mid-July through early September. The ideal time to visit the Marbles is around late June and the Trinities the first half of July. Fall also is a very good time. You'll miss the vivid greens of the meadows and the wildflowers then, of course, but autumn hues have their own unique beauty, too.

The mountains of northwestern California were one of the last portions of the state to be explored by white men. Except for fur trappers, who were active after the late 1820's, the area was pretty much ignored until the discovery of gold at Readings Bar on the Trinity River in 1848. Remains of this past activity are seen today both on the drives to the trailheads and on many of the hikes and with the recent rise in the price of gold, there's been a substantial resurgence in mining.

Speculating on or reading about the origin of names for physical features is an interesting and often informative pastime for hikers. You can make a good guess as to why many landmarks, such as Hidden Lake, are so named. Or, for instance, probably someone saw, or perhaps killed, a large bear near what became known as Big Bear Lake. The bruin that inspired the naming of Grizzly Lake actually may not have been an *Ursus horribilis*. Apparently, prospectors tended to call all bears grizzlies. (Farmers usually were more discerning.) Incidentally, over 200 place names in California honor the grizzly. Coffee Creek may have been so named because a prospector (or his mule) knocked a pot of coffee into it. Places

3

named for people usually are obvious, even if little is known about the individual. Weaverville, originally called Weavertown, was named for a prospector who built the first cabin there in 1850. When the names are corruptions of Indian or other non-English words, the connection often is not so straightforward. Klamath, as in mountains and river, was called "Claminitt" and "Clammitte" until the early 1850's when the current spelling was adopted. The word, in a derivation not entirely obvious to the untutored, came from the Chinook name for a sister tribe, the *Tlamatl*. The name for the Siskiyou Mountains could have come from the Chinook word for bob-tailed horse as a prized one was lost by the leader of a Hudson Bay Company pack train crossing the range in 1828 or it could be from the French *six cailloux* (six stones), the name given to a ford of the Umpqua River by Hudson Bay Company trappers or neither of the above. For much fascinating reading about other place names peruse Erwin Gudde's *California Place Names*.

The 41 hikes and backpacks described in this guide, although they give a representative sampling of the best trails, by no means exhaust the possibilities in northwestern California. If you intend to explore other routes beyond those noted here you should acquire a recreation map for the Klamath, Shasta or Trinity National Forest, depending on which one has jurisdiction over the area you'll be visiting. These maps show the trails and physical features such as streams, lakes, peaks, roads, etc. However, they usually don't have contour lines so you'll need to purchase U.S.G.S. topographic maps for calculating elevation gains and losses, steepness of the terrain and so on. Actually, you should have a recreation map even if you plan to confine your outings to those described in this guide. It affords an overview of the forest and it's fun to keep yourself oriented. The main hiking areas are rather like a hub with the spokes being the trails and the rim the trailheads. So, you can make two hikes that begin scores of miles apart yet end up only one valley away. These recreation maps are $.50 each and you can obtain them from ranger stations or by writing to the National Forest headquarters whose addresses are listed farther on. Be forewarned that just because a trail is shown on a map doesn't mean it's well-defined in the field. Also, unless they are specifically described, such as the loop between Red Rock Vally (No. 5) and Sky High Lakes (No. 4), the potential side and loop trips and extensions mentioned in this guide are only suggested possibilities — they have not been checked by the authors. Because the Marbles and Trinities are such a honeycomb of interconnecting routes, the adventuresome hiker can create many loops.

Permits for day hikes as well as backpacks are required when traveling in a designated wilderness. Whether or not you'll need one for hikes in this guide is so indicated in the information capsule at the beginning of each write-up. These permits are free and you can obtain them ahead of time by mail or in person. If applying by mail give the beginning and ending dates of your trip, points of entry and exit, destination, location of camps (if you're backpacking), number of stock, number of people in your group and your name and address. If you plan to obtain a permit in person be sure to arrive at a ranger station during its operating hours, usually weekdays from 8:00 a.m. to 4:00 p.m. Below are listed the national forests through which trails in this guide travel and the relevant ranger stations. If you're only obtaining a permit all you have to be concerned with is writing or visiting the right national forest. However, when you want specific information about a trail or area, you should talk with people at the ranger station in charge of the region you'll be visiting. For example, it's not the job of the people at the Oak Knoll District Ranger Station to know what's happening on the routes from Coffee Creek Road. Getting precisely the correct ranger station by mail is not so crucial as your query will be forewarded if you've sent it to the wrong one.

Klamath National Forest
1215 S. Main Street
Yreka, California 96097

      Oak Knoll District Ranger Station
      Klamath River, California 96039
        Trails No's. 1 and 2

Scott River District Ranger Station
Fort Jones, California 96032
    Trail No's. 3 through 9
    Trail No's. 13 through 17

        for Trail No's 3 through 9 you also can visit the
        Kelsey Creek Ranger Station

        for Trails No's. 13 through 17 you also can visit the
        Callahan Ranger Station.

Salmon River District Ranger Station
Sawyers Bar, California 96027
    Trail No's. 10 through 12
        for Trail No's. 10 through 12 you also can visit the
        Forks of Salmon Ranger Station

Shasta-Trinity National Forest
1615 Continental Street
Redding, California 96001

    Coffee Creek Ranger Station
    (mailing address: Trinity Center, California 96091)
        Trail No's. 19 through 30

    Weaverville District Ranger Station
    Weaverville, California 96093
        Trail No's. 31 through 35
            for Trail No's. 31 through 35 you also can visit the
            Mule Creek Ranger Station

    Ranger Station
    Junction City, California 96048
        Trail No's. 36 through 38

    Ranger Station
    204 Alma Street
    Mt. Shasta City, California 96067
        Trail No's. 18, 39 and 40

Obtaining permits is a bit of a bother, of course, but the Forest Service uses information from them to determine management policies.

Although the final miles to many of the trailheads are along unpaved roads, none is extremely rough or steep. Keep in mind, though, that travel on routes such as California 3 or Forest Highway 93 is slower than on a freeway and that progress is even slower on unpaved roads.

Regarding water, hikers and backpackers can be divided into three groups: those who drink from any source but the most obviously polluted; those who purify *everything*; and those in between who take well informed, calculated risks. The majority follow the middle course and only drink untreated water from side streams they know don't come from lakes where much camping occurs or flow through areas open to grazing. To what extent you drink untreated water is your decision. Speaking of grazing, be forewarned that the surface dryness of manure mounds often belies their interior consistency.

And, speaking of water, the stream crossings on trails described in this guide and throughout the high country of northwestern California in general seldom are a problem. The largest of them are bridged and the few fords that are so deep you can't prevent getting your feet wet aren't risky except in times of freshet. However, never risk fording a stream you feel is dangerous. When you come to one of those few crossings that are too deep to hop from rock to rock, you have three acceptable options: take off your boots and socks and wear the tennis shoes you've farsightedly packed; remove boots only, wade across in your socks and wring them out thoroughly on the other side; wear only your boots. For the first two it's a good idea to put your boots in your pack or securely tie them on your pack because if you stumble your first reflex will be to drop them. Don't ford barefoot as it's too easy to bruise or cut your feet and you're increasing your chance of blisters with both wet socks and boots.

Sometimes it's your upper body, not feet, you're concerned about keeping dry. Although the rainfall in northwestern California isn't excessive it does come, both during occasional afternoon thunderstorms as well as from frontal activity. Rather than wearing flapping ponchos that trap your body heat and cause you to get as wet from perspiration as from precipitation, carry a man's large umbrella when rain is possible. It keeps your head, torso, pack (and glasses, if you wear them) dry and it's not tiring to hold. (Ponchos still are best while performing camp chores.) Make sure you're off peaks and exposed ridges when a thunderstorm breaks and don't stand under a lone tree. From observing scarred trunks, it's obvious that lightning strikes aren't limited to the highest areas but, statistically, your risks are lessened when you're on lower, wooded slopes.

Another recommended accouterment is a walking cane. It's a welcome third leg while fording streams and traversing rough terrain and can give relief to grumbling knees on steep downhill grades. Hikers with strong upper arms even use a cane to help propel themselves uphill faster. Buy a model with a curved handle so you can hook it over your wrist when you need your hands free. If your local outdoor stores don't stock them, you can purchase a cane at surgical supply houses.

Whether you're hiking or backpacking, be sure to include adequate clothing. An accident can happen, even on the smoothest trail, and mountain weather can become nasty very quickly. Always include a wool hat, gloves, sweater, a windbreaker and poncho or some other waterproof garment. A flashlight, first aid kit, whistle, map of the area and extra food also should be standard equipment.

Rattlesnakes certainly inhabit northwestern California but their density along the trails is such that on the hikes done by the authors for this and an earlier guide they actually saw three (two of those in Morris Meadows on the trek to Emerald and Sapphire Lakes No. 33) and the third on the Bear Creek Trail No. 38 where they also heard two others. Despite the low odds of encountering these reptiles, preventive measures still are wise, the most important being to scan the trail ahead while hiking and checking the immediate area before getting water or sitting down. Read how to treat a snake bite. A few years ago a recommended procedure was to put the bitten limb or area in a cold stream or in ice. This supposedly slowed the spread of the venom. However, it also retarded the body's ability to break down the toxic proteins and was found to encourage gangrene. Remember that rattlesnakes are not aggressive. The problem is they also are not quick. So you have to be alert enough that you or it have time to retreat. Don't molest or kill them. After all, they're year around residents and you're just a visitor.

Because of heavier use and the expectations most people have when they visit the backcountry, it's most important that hikers and backpackers have impeccable outdoor manners. Litter is blessedly scarce but if you see any pick it up and pack it out. Although organic, orange rinds, egg shells and such decompose with glacial rapidity so don't leave them behind. What you do leave are wildflowers and other plants. Never, ever pick them — those who follow want to enjoy them, too. Don't be part of a large group — sheep and cattle are supposed to be in herds, not people. While hiking, stay on the established treads. Don't shortcut switchbacks. Doing so occasionally is dangerous to those below but the primary reason is that it creates unsightly erosion channels. Money spent repairing these unnecessary gulleys could be much better used to maintain existing routes. If you hike early in the season also try to stay on the official alignment when crossing melting snow patches. The ground is especially vulnerable then and avoiding a lingering snow patch over the trail leaves side paths that are a long time healing.

Aural, as well as visual, pollution doesn't belong in the wilderness. Shouting, radios, barking dogs, etc. definitely aren't appropriate and most people would prefer listening to the sounds of wind in the trees or the rush of a nearby stream than someone's unnatural flute or guitar.

Backpackers, because of their greater impact, have to be even more aware of their actions. The Golden Rule for them, as well as day hikers, is "Be Inconspicuous." The phrase the Forest Service currently is using is "No Trace Camping." It means just that: you should leave no trace of having visited the area. You shouldn't dig trenches or hip holes; you should use primus type stoves instead of gleaning every spicule of wood and building fires that scar the ground; you should properly dispose of body wastes and camp at least 200 feet from streams and lakes. More subtle aspects of No Trace Camping are scattering a few cones and other appropriate debris over your camp area just before you leave so it appears more natural and buying earth-toned, rather than vivid red and orange or similarly hued, clothing and equipment so you blend in with the landscape. Little brochures on proper hiking and backpacking techniques usually are given out with permits or are on display at ranger stations. Be sure to study them and follow their tenets.

Backcountry management is not unchanging and not all the places visited by the trails in this guide are in designated wilderness areas. Your informed input about future use of the region is important. Talk with or write to the appropriate national forests or ranger districts for information. Support their policies if you approve and object if you don't. For more information on conservation matters contact the Sierra Club, 530 Bush Street, San Francisco, California 94108. Comments intended for the authors can be sent to them in care of The Touchstone Press, P.O. Box 81, Beaverton, Oregon 97075.

Good Hiking!

D.L.
R.L.

Mount Shasta

area map

*shaded area covered by
detail map page 11*

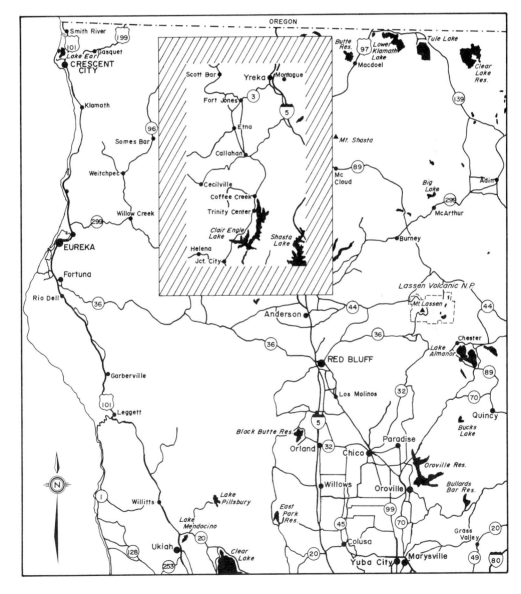

The "Happy Bear" above Sky High Lakes

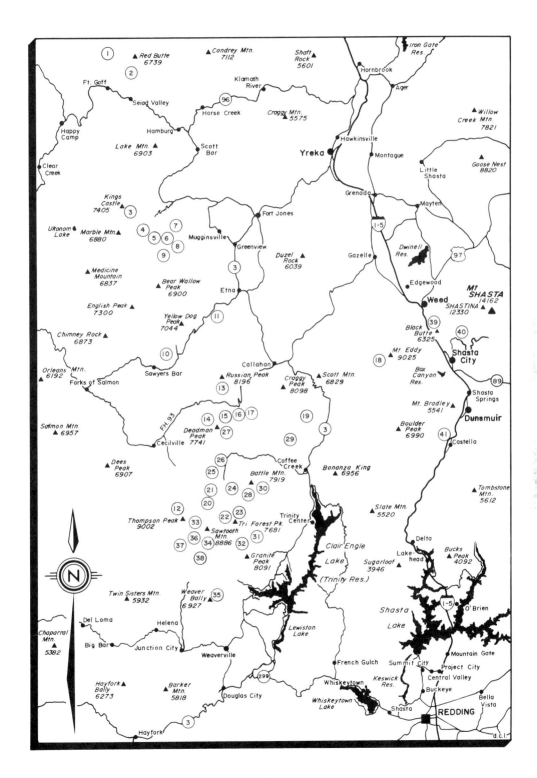

Castle Crags from Castle Dome Trail

contents

LEGEND

⬢	Starting Point
– – – –	Trail
· · · · · · ·	Obscure Trail
△	Campsite
◼ ◣	Building or Remains
5.0	Mileage
No. 9W14	Trail No.
4S02	Road No.
⌁	Bridge
◼═ ═	Access Road

1 LONESOME LAKE

Backpack
Distance: 12.5 miles one way
Elevation gain: 4,340 feet; loss 100 feet
Allow 6½ to 8 hours one way
Usually open late May through October
High Point: 5,580 feet
Topographic map:
  U.S.G.S. Happy Camp, Calif.-Oreg.
  15'   **1956**

No Permit Required

Seiad Valley borders the Klamath River about 50 miles west of I-5 and two hikes in the area, one a day trip to Lower Devils Peak (No. 2) and the considerably longer trek to Lonesome Lake, are described in this guide. These two hikes are by no means the only ones along the north slope of the valley: the Portuguese Creek Trail and a recently rebuilt section of the Pacific Crest Trail begin in the area and the Bounday Trail traverses west a bit below the crest of the Siskiyou Mountains from the Pacific Crest Trail near Kangaroo Mountain. Begin all of these hikes with adaquate water. Because of the high temperatures after early June, the Seiad Valley area is most comfortably visited in the late spring or fall. Unfortunately, ticks and poison oak are plentiful.

Most of the long, gradual to moderate climb to Lonesome Lake is through attractive woods. Near the destination the view includes Goff Butte, Rattlesnake Mountain, Mt. Emily and Red Butte and extends south to the tips of the Marble Mountains.

Proceed on I-5 about 11 miles north of Yreka to the Klamath River Highway exit. Head south on a section of the old highway for 2.5 miles to a junction just before a bridge. Keep right on California 96, the Klamath River Highway, and drive 44.5 miles to the town of Seiad Valley. Continue west 4.2 miles to a sign on your right at the east end of the Fort Goff Cemetery that identifies the beginning of the Fort Goff Trail. Parking is available at the Fort Goff Public Campground 75 feet farther west off the south side of the highway.

Walk east for 200 yards, switchback left and continue uphill. Briefly traverse a steep, open slope then cross a road and hike at a gradual grade along the wall of the wooded canyon holding Fort Goff Creek. Begin walking along a section of a broad old road, following it downhill from time to time. Cross a side stream and travel beside the shore of Fort Goff Creek for several yards then continue along the road that occasionally is washed out or so overgrown it resembles a trail. Eventually, however, the roadbed ends and the trail proper begins.

Traverse at a more noticeable grade along the narrow valley wall just above the creek. Cross a side stream at 2.9 miles and soon begin climbing away from the canyon floor. Pass a cluster of azalea bushes and farther on enjoy many other wildflowers if you make the trip in late spring. At 4.8 miles cross a robust stream in a small side canyon and 1.2 miles farther come to Big Camp, both good choices for a rest stop. Walk almost on the level for 0.4 mile beyond Big Camp to the crossing of the East Fork of Goff Creek. Go upstream a few feet from the ford then switchback. One-quarter mile farther cross another stream and pass a path on your left down to Sugar Pine Camp. Continue climbing through woods void of ground cover for 0.5 mile to the junction of the route to the Portuguese Creek Trail and Cook and Green Pass.

Keep left and climb to the northwest at a gradual grade. The vegetation becomes increasingly sparse and at 10.0 miles the trail traverses the upper, brushy slopes of Goff Butte. Come to a saddle on its west shoulder, climb along the ridge crest then descend through open timber to the former site of Bailey's Cabin. Resume climbing, come to the ridge top and walk along the crest in a westerly direction then descend for a few hundred yards to Lonesome Lake.

14

Fort Goff Creek

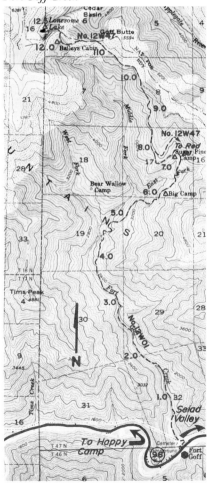

2 LOWER DEVILS PEAK

One day trip
Distance: 5 miles one way
Elevation gain: 3,670 feet
Allow 3½ to 4½ hours one way
Usually open May through mid-November
High Point: 5,040 feet
Topographic map:
   U.S.G.S. Seiad Valley, Calif.
   15'   1955

No Permit Required

The view from the summit of Lower Devils Peak extends southeast to Mt. Shasta (see No. 40), south to the tips of the Marble Mountains and west as far as Preston Peak and its neighbors. Seiad Valley lies directly below, while the distinctively colored Red Butte and the slash of the trail past Middle and Upper Devils Peaks are closer across the steep, treeless canyon to the north. The mix of manzanita, deer brush, madrone, oak, pine and other vegetation that thrives on the drier, warmer slopes of Lower Devils Peak are a contrast to the lusher woods encountered on the hike to Lonesome Lake (No. 1), the other trail from Seiad Valley described in this guide. Watch for poison oak beside the trail and check your clothing periodically for ticks. Begin the hike with adequate water.

Drive on I-5 about 11 miles north of Yreka to the Klamath River Highway exit. Head south on a section of the old highway for 2.5 miles to a junction just before a bridge across the river. Keep right on California 96, the Klamath River Highway, and proceed 44.5 miles to the town of Seiad Valley. Beyond the west end of the community pass a sign on the right (north) side of the road stating School House Gulch and continue 0.2 mile farther on the highway to a marker, again on your right, indicating the beginning of the Lower Devils Peak Lookout Trail. A large turnout is opposite the trailhead off the south side of the highway.

Walk up the rutted, old roadbed for 20 feet, curve left then after 150 yards veer left from the road onto a path. Wind up over rocky, mostly open terrain for 0.2 mile then begin traversing along a smooth surface that prevails, with only a few short exceptions, for the remainder of the climb. Head generally east then near 0.3 mile at the junction of an abandoned path where a sign states *Trail* turn left and continue up a steady, moderate grade in a northwesterly direction. Curve sharply right at 1.0 mile and after 200 yards come to the cistern at Fern Springs. Continue traversing through woods then curve left into a large side canyon and travel along its western wall. Make several irregular switchbacks then near 1.7 miles pass an unmarked side path on your left that descends 75 feet to a spring that dries up later in the summer.

Continue climbing at a steady, moderate grade in irregular switchbacks. Lower Devils Peak is visible periodically and on the last traverse to the west the dark bulk of Preston Peak comes into view. Curve right and traverse the northwest facing wall of another large side canyon. The character of the vegetation reflects the moister, more shaded nature of this slope.

Near 3.0 miles come to the crest of the ridge, turn left and wind up then traverse just below it. Briefly rejoin the crest and climb at a steeper grade. Switchback to a small saddle and resume traversing then make 13 switchbacks, passing a signed side path to a spring near the last one. This spur descends for about 150 yards to a barrel that is filled year around. Walk along the crest on the main trail, veer right and continue to the site of a former lookout. Lumber from the building was taken away by helicopter a few years ago and Forest Service personnel are considering blasting the foundation. If you want to hike farther, walk back along the trail from the lookout about 150 feet to an unsigned junction and veer right. Seiad, originally spelled Sciad, may be a corruption of an Indian word for "far-away land".

16

Survey marker near the Lookout

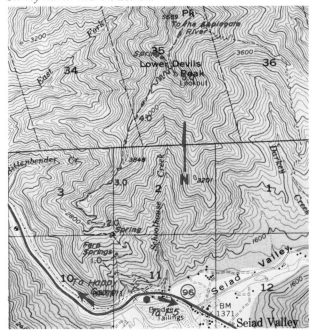

3 PARADISE LAKE

One day trip or backpack
Distance: 6.8 miles one way
Elevation gain: 3,800 feet
Allow 4 to 5 hours one way
Usually open June through October
High Point: 6,150 feet
Topographic map:
  U.S.G.S. Scott Bar, Calif.
  15'   1955

Permit Required

Passing through different vegetation zones is a standard bonus on hikes with meaningful elevation gains and the trip up the length of the Kelsey Creek valley to Paradise Lake is no exception. The trek begins in woods predominantly of oak and pine and ends in fir-rimmed meadows, lush with grass and that ubiquitous false hellebore. You can continue above timberline by making the short side trip of 1.2 miles with 700 feet of additional uphill to the interestingly rocky and barren ridge above Bear Lake. Experienced hikers can descend from this crest past Turk Lake and rejoin the main trail at the 5.2 or 6.0 mile points.

At the south end of Fort Jones turn north onto signed Scott River Road and follow it 17 miles to a bridge just beyond the spur that heads east up to the Kelsey Creek Guard Station. Cross the span and immediately turn left onto an unpaved and possibly unsigned road. Follow it for 0.7 mile, keeping straight where a spur heads down on the left, to the signed trailhead.

After 150 feet switchback once then climb gradually through woods for 0.8 mile and keep straight (right) at a faint junction on your left of the path along Cayenne Ridge to Paradise Lake. Initially, you'll be paralleling an abandoned canal on your right, a remnant of past mining activity. Rise more noticeably for 0.3 mile to the junction on the face of the slope of the also faint path up to Stud Horse Camp.

Continue straight along the main trail at an erratic grade, generally traveling directly above Kelsey Creek. At 2.0 miles pass above a camp area, just beyond it climb in four switchbacks and resume traversing up at a steeper grade. Make two short switchbacks and a few tenths mile farther ford the North Fork of Kelsey Creek in a good sized canyon. By this point the woods have become predominantly coniferous.

Continue uphill, cross a small stream and at 3.9 miles pass Maple Falls. Climb at a noticeably steeper angle for awhile, cross another flow and continue up to the largest side stream yet a few yards before a fence and gate. Soon come to a meadow and near its middle, at 5.2 miles, pass a sign on the ground identifying the path to Turk and Bear Lakes.

Keep in the same direction you were heading and at the far end of the clearing enter a finger of woods. Cross the outlet from Turk Lake and then walk through more meadows. Begin traversing up along the north side of the valley to its head, crossing several side streams. After one switchback come to the bench holding Paradise Lake that reposes below the rocky outcropping of Kings Castle. Signs near the outlet stream identify the Pacific Crest Trail No. 2000 that enters the Marble Valley (see No. 4) 5.0 miles to the south and heads north to Big Ridge.

To make the recommended side trip or loop, head north, cross the outlet and follow well-defined No. 2000. Traverse along the valley wall, crossing two side streams with the second being a good spot for a snack stop. Enter coniferous woods and then contour along more open slopes to a rocky crest. Travel on the level and descend along the ridge, eventually having a view left down onto Bear Lake, to a four-way junction. Turn right, get a good bearing on Turk Lake, wind down over the rough, rocky trail and then continue descending in a traverse. The trail is faint on either side of a meadow a short distance before the lake. The trail from Turk Lake down to the junction with the main route at 5.2 miles is obscure and the well-defined tread that heads south and crosses the outlet eventually peters out. Follow whichever one you locate first and if you lose it merely head down until you intersect No. 11W12.

18

Paradise Lake and the Kings Castle

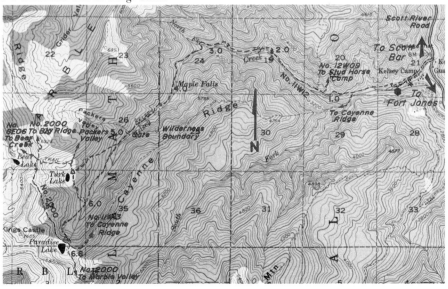

4 SKY HIGH LAKES

One day trip or backpack
Distance: 5.5 miles one way
Elevation gain: 1,580 feet; loss 100 feet
Allow 3 to 3½ hours one way
Usually open June through October
High Point: 5,800 feet
Topographic map:
  U.S.G.S. Scott Bar, Calif.
  15'   1955

Permit Required

Three hikes (this one to Sky High Lakes, No. 5 to Red Rock Valley and No. 6 to Deep Lake) begin from Lovers Camp. Because of the interlocking network of trails in the Marble Mountain Wilderness, you can visit all three eminently attractive destinations in one backpack and also travel north to Paradise Lake (No. 3), east to Wright (No. 7), Calf (No. 8) and Campbell and Cliff (No. 9) Lakes plus other scenic places in the preserve.

On the hike to Sky High Lakes you have the option of two return loops. The shorter, which adds 2.3 miles and 600 feet uphill, travels through Little Marble Valley then rejoins the trail you followed in. The longer returns through Red Rock Valley. This latter loop would be a total of 12 miles with 2,400 feet of elevation gain.

At the south end of Fort Jones turn north onto the signed road to Scott River and Bar and follow it 14 miles to a large sign pointing to Canyon Creek Access Road and listing several mileages. Turn left, cross a bridge and keep left at the entrance to Indian Scotty Campground. Three-quarters mile farther along the unpaved road stay right on 44N45 where a spur heads left to the Wrights Lake Trail. After 4.0 miles turn left, proceed 2.0 miles more, pass a camp area then continue the final several hundred feet to the road's

end at a large parking lot with water and toilet facilities.

The hike begins from the south end of the parking area and is identified by a sign stating Canyon Creek Trail. Climb then drop slightly along an old roadbed to a sheltered bulletin board. Continue through woods as the old bed narrows to a trail, pass the Wilderness boundary marker and at 0.4 mile come to the junction of the trails to Red Rock Valley and Deep Lake.

Keep right, after several yards curve sharply right and begin climbing along a sometimes rough tread. Cross a small side stream, continue uphill and then drop slightly to Death Valley Creek at 1.2 miles. Soon resume climbing, but at a gentler grade, to Big Rock Creek at 2.0 miles. Continue rising gradually through an interesting forest of conifers, big maples and abundant dogwood.

Around 3.0 miles the grade becomes steeper and the tread rocky. Keep left at the junction of a trail to the Marble Valley Guard Station, cross two streams and continue up to a second route to the guard station. Stay left and after 75 feet keep left a third time at a path to Little Marble Valley. Wind uphill, traverse above a bowl to a gate, beyond which is an overview of Gate Lake. From the crest above this small lake wind down briefly along a rocky ridge to a stream crossing and then mosey up across terrain of bushes, grass and scattered trees. Pass the abandoned trail to Red Rock Valley on your left and continue up to a big grassy area. Keep left to reach a shelter and stay right to visit Lower Sky High Lake.

Even if you don't intend to make either of the loops, continue beyond Lower Sky High Lake along the trail that skirts the western end of Frying Pan Lake and climb a bit for an overview of the basin. If you are doing one of the circuits, keep climbing to the junction of Trail No. 2000 on the ridge crest. Turn left to return through Red Rock Valley (see No. 5 for details). To make the shorter loop, turn right. Follow the crest for about 0.3 mile to a junction, take the far right trail and descend in a few switchbacks into the woods on the west side of Little Marble Valley. Keep left at the junction of the spur trail on your right and continue down through woods and around large boulders to the Marble Valley Guard Station. Take the trail on the right that continues down through woods, keep left at the first junction and a short distance farther meet the trail you followed in.

Frying Pan Lake

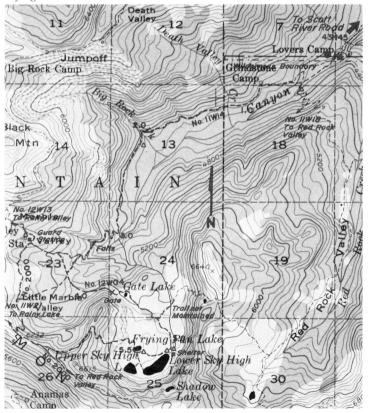

5 RED ROCK VALLEY

One day trip or backpack
Distance: 4.1 miles one way
Elevation gain: 1,720 feet; loss 100 feet
Allow 2½ to 3 hours one way
Usually open June through October
High Point: 6,000 feet
Topographic map:
  U.S.G.S. Scott Bar, Calif.
  15'   1955

Permit Required

The hike up through the woods, huge meadows and open expanses of Red Rock Valley is the middle of the three routes that begin from Lovers Camp. A delightful loop is possible by climbing the head of the valley and then traveling west along a ridge crest to a connector down to Sky High Lakes (No. 4) and descending along Trail 11W14 to the junction with the route you followed in at 0.4 mile. This circuit would involve a total of 12 miles and 2,400 feet of elevation gain. The first 2.8 miles of the hike to Red Rock Valley is the same as the one to Little Elk and Deep Lakes (No. 6).

At the south end of Fort Jones turn north onto the signed road to Scott River and Bar and follow it 14 miles to a large sign pointing to Canyon Creek Access Road and listing several mileages. Turn left, cross a bridge and keep left at the entrance to Indian Scotty Campground. Three-quarters mile farther along the unpaved road keep right on 44N45 where a spur heads left to the Wright Lakes Trail (No. 7). After 4.0 miles turn left, proceed 2.0 miles more, pass a camp area then continue the final several hundred feet to the large parking lot with water and toilets.

The hike begins from the south end of the parking area on the Canyon Creek Trail. Climb then drop slightly along an old road-bed to a sheltered bulletin board. Continue through woods as the bed narrows to a trail. Pass the Wilderness boundary marker and at 0.4 mile come to the junction of the trail to Sky High Lakes, the one you'll be taking back if you make the recommended loop.

Turn left and walk 40 yards to the crossing of Canyon Creek. Look upstream for a possible log crossing, although a replacement could be in a different location. Climb moderately in two switchbacks separated by long traverses then travel along the east side of a ridge. Pass through an area of grass and false hellebore, climb and then descend slightly to a clearing rimmed by willows. Go through a fringe of trees to a big meadow and near its southern end pass a cabin. Ford a wide, but shallow, stream and continue on the level a bit farther then resume climbing in woods. Level off, drop slightly and come to a more open area at the confluence of two branches of Red Rock Creek.

Although the trail up Red Rock Valley is to the west (right) of the creek, during high water it's usually easier to cross the main flow on your left and then recross it just south of (above) the confluence. The trail to Deep Lake travels along the valley floor after the first crossing for a short distance then winds up the east wall. Pass a camp area on an island between the two flows and after several yards cross the side branch.

Climb along the length of a massive meadow to a stream crossing at its upper end. Beyond a band of woods come to another open area dotted with deciduous trees, including aspen, and conifers. Cross a small stream in a finger of evergreens then rise more steeply to rock outcroppings near the head of the valley. After an easy ford of a good sized stream, move into woods and pass above a pond inhabited by noisy frogs. Traverse west and then resume winding up to the ridge crest and the junction with No. 2000, the Pacific Crest Trail.

To visit Sky High Lakes, turn right and walk along the crest. Pass a sign pointing right to Shadow Lake, which soon comes into view. Continue downhill to a trail on the right and a possibly obscure sign pointing to Sky High Lakes. Keep right and several yards farther at the crest keep right again and continue down to the northeast, soon having your first view of Frying Pan and Upper and Lower Sky High Lakes.

22

The Stockman's Cabin

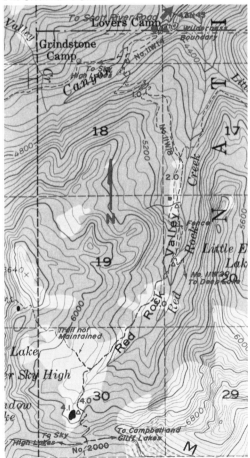

6 DEEP LAKE

One day trip or backpack
Distance: 7.8 miles one way
Elevation gain: 2,800 feet; loss 900 feet
Allow 4½ to 5½ hours one way
Usually open June through October
High Point: 6,340 feet
Topographic map:
  U.S.G.S. Scott Bar, Calif.
  15'   1955

Permit Required

The trip to Deep Lake is one that affords several options: it shares the same alignment with the route to Red Rock Valley (No. 5) for the initial 2.8 miles and you can continue up through the length of the valley as a scenic side hike. If you want a shorter trip of 4.3 miles one way with a total elevation gain of 1,680 feet you could turn around at Little Elk Lake, an entirely satisfying destination. For those who, instead, want a longer outing, a less well-defined trail heads 4.0 miles south from Little Elk Lake to Campbell and Cliff Lakes (No. 9) and another contours for 3.0 miles from Deep Lake to Wright Lakes (No. 7).

At the south end of Fort Jones turn north onto the signed road to Scott River and Bar and follow it 14 miles to a large sign pointing to Canyon Creek Access Road and listing several mileages. Turn left, cross a bridge and keep left at the entrance to Indian Scotty Campground. Three-quarters mile farther along the unpaved road keep right on 44N45 where a spur heads left to the Wright Lakes Trail. After 4.0 miles turn left, proceed 2.0 miles more, pass a camp area then continue

the final several hundred feet to a large parking lot with water and toilet facilities.

The hike begins from the south end of the parking area on the Canyon Creek Trail. Climb then drop slightly along an old roadbed to a sheltered bulletin board. Continue through woods along the old bed that soon narrows to a trail, pass the Wilderness boundary marker and at 0.4 mile come to the junction of the trail to Sky High Lakes (No. 4).

Turn left and walk 40 yards to the crossing of Canyon Creek. Look upstream for a possible log crossing. Climb moderately in two switchbacks separated by long traverses then travel along the east side of a ridge. Pass through a wee area of grass and false hellebore, climb and then descend slightly to a clearing rimmed by willows. Go through a fringe of trees to a big meadow and near its southern end pass a cabin. Ford a wide, shallow stream and continue on the level a bit farther then resume climbing in woods. Level off, drop slightly and come to a more open area at the confluence of two branches of Red Rock Valley Creek.

Turn left, leaving the trail that continues up through the remainder of the valley, and ford the combined flows. When the water is high, try downstream for a better crossing. Continue up the valley a short distance and then curve left and wind up in eight rocky switchbacks that become increasingly shorter. As you gain elevation, you'll have views down into the Red Rock Valley. At the ridge top begin gradually descending northeast and parallel to the crest for 0.2 mile then descend along the east facing slope to Little Elk Lake on the floor of a small valley.

To continue the hike to Deep Lake, walk along the north shore, cross the outlet creek to a sign identifying Trail 11W20. Turn left, following the sign to Deep Lake, and begin climbing. Cross beneath a graceful stairstep waterfall then rise along steeply sloped open areas that frequently afford good views west to the colored walls above Red Rock Valley and to Marble Mountain.

The trail becomes level at about 6.0 miles where it reenters woods and begins gradually curving east and then south. Descend, cross an open area with several small creeks and climb a short distance to the northeast past a grassy meadow. Switchback to the south, pass the junction of the new trail to Wright Lakes and climb for the final mile at a steady grade above a luxuriant marsh to the edge of Deep Lake.

Meadow near Deep Lake

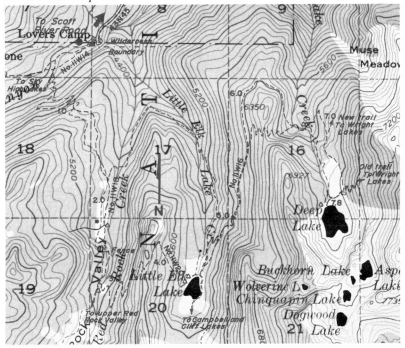

7 WRIGHT LAKES

One day trip or backpack
Distance: 5 miles one way
Elevation gain: 2,600 feet
Allow 3 to 4 hours one way
Usually open late June through October
High Point: 7,400 feet
Topographic map:
  U.S.G.S. Scott Bar, Calif.
  15'   1955

Permit Required

The high lakes in the Marble Mountains, and throughout much of California for that matter, are noted for the fine fishing they afford and the Wright Lakes have been among the best. Another common feature of the Marbles, abundantly represented on this hike, is the profusion of false hellebore. If you hike frequently in these mountains, you'll come to consider the plant a friend after you've observed uncounted thousands progress through their life cycle. They begin as tight spirals — rather like little, green furled umbrellas — poking through the moist ground in spring and slowly unwinding as they mature. If you pass an adult patch, particularly when in bloom, you'll understand why the plants also are called corn lilies. Unfortunately, false hellebore tends to quickly take over meadows. Livestock don't like it and, in fact, the roots are poisonous to them.

A section of the tread is faint or nonexistent beyond 4.3 miles so, although the terrain itself presents no problems, you should be prepared for a bit of cross-country travel.

At the south end of Fort Jones turn north onto the signed road to Scott River and Bar and follow it 14 miles to a large sign pointing to Canyon Creek Access Road and listing several mileages. Turn left, cross a bridge and keep left at the entrance to Indian Scotty Campground. Three-quarters mile farther along the unpaved road keep left at the junction of the road to Lovers Camp and the start of hike No's. 4, 5 and 6. Follow 44N53 for 1.8 miles to where the bed is blocked by a dirt mound. This is about 100 feet beyond (west of) the third switchback on 44N53.

Walk along the road for 1.7 miles to where an obvious trail heads up on the left. This junction is about 0.3 mile beyond the second switchback you've made since you began hiking. Switchback up the wooded northeast facing slope then taper off and travel near the crest of the ridge. At 2.2 miles pass the Wilderness boundary and soon begin winding up the nose of the main ridge for 0.5 mile. Leave the woods and traverse an open slope on the northwest side of the ridge. Switchback once to the left and continue rising to the crest at a big rock spire. You can see west to Marble Mountain and Kings Castle above Paradise Lake (No. 3). Switchback once and travel at a gradual uphill grade along the sparsely wooded slope for 0.3 mile to the junction of the trail that descends for 2.2 miles to Deep Lake (No. 6).

Keep left, drop briefly then enter deep woods and near 3.9 miles pass through a scraggy, rocky area. Soon leave the heavy timber for the last time and traverse into a side canyon holding Boulder Creek. Note precisely where you ford the creek as the route from the east bank is faint or may be nonexistent. After you cross Boulder Creek climb through an immense field of false hellebore for about 30 yards then curve right and walk through marshy terrain. Go over a slight rise and then come to the bench that extends north from Lower Wright Lake.

To make the 0.4 mile extension to Upper Wright Lake, follow one of several side paths that start near the northeastern shore of the lower lake. About three-quarters of the way up to the crest take the right fork where the trail splits or you'll have to walk several hundred yards cross-country and downhill to reach the lake.

A trail follows along the northern and eastern shore to a grassy slope then winds up it to the crest and the junction of the trail north and east to Big Meadows and south to Boulder Peak and Campbell Lake (No. 9). For a scenic little side trip turn right and head south along the crest for about 0.2 mile then turn upslope and climb to the cliffs overlooking Lower Wright Lake.

Lower Wright Lake

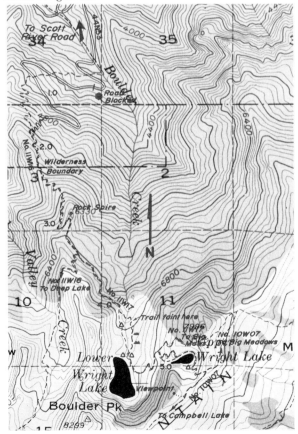

8   CALF LAKE

One day trip or backpack
Distance: 5 miles one way
Elevation gain: 2,220 feet
Allow 3 hours one way
Usually open June through October
High Point: 7,000 feet
Topographic map:
   U.S.G.S. Scott Bar, Calif.
   15'   1955

Permit Required

The hikes to Calf Lake and to Campbell and Cliff Lakes (No. 9) share the same tread for the first 2.8 miles but beyond that point the two trips are remarkably different in their scenic attributes: the route to the latter two travels through alpine terrain whereas the climb up to the head of the little valley holding Calf Lake is in a more varied, though no less attractive, landscape before reaching the usual lake setting of grass, scattered trees, boulders and rock walls.

At the south end of Fort Jones turn north onto the signed road to Scott River and Bar and follow it for 7.0 miles to the Quartz Valley Road. Turn left onto the latter and after 4.0 miles come to a signed junction on your right of the road to Shackleford and Big Meadows. The Quartz Valley Road continues south and east for about 6.0 miles to where it meets California 3 near the community of Green-

view 5.0 miles south of Fort Jones.

Turn west onto unpaved Road 43N21 and after 2.0 miles, just beyond a stream crossing, keep straight then less than a mile farther curve left, continuing on 43N21. After 3.0 miles stay left at the junction of Big Meadows Road and drive the final 2.0 miles to a large parking area below on your left. A few parking spaces are at the actual trailhead but, everything considered, it's easier to begin from the lower site.

Walk (or drive) along 43N21 for 0.5 mile to the beginning of the Shackleford Creek Trail at a switchback. Cross many side streams along the first several hundred yards, continue at an almost level grade through woods and across small clearings and creeks for a pleasant 2.1 miles then begin climbing in earnest. Eventually, have a short respite, climb to a stream crossing, level off and walk along the edge of a clearing to the junction of the trail to Campbell and Cliff Lakes.

Turn right, travel on the level to a stream crossing and then wind up through less imposing woods for about 0.3 mile to a second, smaller ford. Level off and come to a stream at the edge of a clearing. Cross the flow and then the meadow to a cabin around which campsites are plentiful. This wooded area is frequented by deer that seem indifferent to the presence of humans.

To continue the hike, keep the side of the cabin on your left and head uphill. The tread becomes obvious again beyond the camp. Rise at an erratic grade through woods to a small grassy area then come to a larger one. At its far side resume climbing along a wooded slope with little ground cover to the junction of the trail to Black Meadows. The remaining distance to Calf Lake is 1.0 mile, not 2.0 as given on the sign.

Turn left and climb steeply. Eventually, travel for a few hundred feet along a ridge crest where grass has replaced the cover of manzanita then veer right into a sparsely wooded little side valley. Continue to a second parallel valley where you'll have a good view of Mt. Shasta. Cross the stream flowing along its floor and then head uphill toward the head of the valley. The tread is faint for the last several yards as it travels over rocks but the location of the lake is obvious. The area around Calf Lake, though visually pleasing, is not suitable for camping. For a short side trip, you can continue for 0.3 mile with 250 feet of elevation gain to small Long High Lake on the bench above to the northeast.

Calf Lake

9 CAMPBELL and CLIFF LAKES

One day trip or backpack
Distance: 4.6 miles one way
Elevation gain: 1,320 feet
Allow 2½ to 3 hours one way
Usually open June through October
High Point: 6,100 feet
Topographic map:
  U.S.G.S. Scott Bar, Calif.
  15'   1955

Permit Required

After visiting Campbell and Cliff Lakes you can make a scenic loop past Summit Lake that would add only 1.2 miles and 450 feet of extra uphill. You also could make a 2.0 mile side trip to Calf Lake (No. 8) or from Summit Lake head north to Marble Valley (see No. 4) or Little Elk Lake (see No. 6). Campsites are plentiful in the Campbell, Cliff and Summit Lakes areas.

At the south end of Fort Jones turn north onto the signed road to Scott River and Bar and follow it for 7.0 miles to the Quartz Valley Road. Turn left onto the latter and after 4.0 miles come to a signed junction on your right to Shackleford and Big Meadows. The Quartz Valley Road continues south and east for about 6.0 miles to where it meets California 3 near the community of Greenview 5.0 miles south of Fort Jones.

Turn west onto unpaved Road 43N21 and after 2.0 miles, just beyond a stream crossing, keep straight then less than a mile farther curve left, continuing on 43N21. After 3.0 miles stay left at the junction of Big Meadows Road and drive the final 2.0 miles to a large parking area below on your left. A few parking spaces are at the actual trailhead but, everything considered, it's easier to begin from the lower site.

Walk (or drive) along 43N21 for 0.5 mile to the beginning of the Shackleford Creek Trail at a switchback. Cross many side streams along the first several hundred yards, continue at an almost level grade through woods and across small clearings and creeks for a pleasant 2.1 miles then begin climbing in earnest. Eventually, have a short respite, climb to a stream crossing, level off and walk along the edge of a clearing to the junction of the trail to Calf Lake.

Keep straight (left) and after several hundred feet walk above Log Lake. Cross a wide swath of weathered avalanche debris, reenter woods, travel along the edge of a large clearing and then beside a stream to the next junction. You'll return on the trail to the right if you make the recommended loop.

Keep left, cross the shallow stream and soon ford two more flows. Leave the level, open terrain and begin climbing along the wooded slope in irregular switchbacks. Level off and come to an unsigned fork of a path that drops to a swampy meadow. Turn left and after several hundred feet come to a junction of a route around the north and northwest sides of Campbell Lake. To stay on the main route, turn right and then keep straight where a path descends to that swampy meadow and connects with the first one you passed. Several hundred feet farther come to the junction of the trail to Summit Lake.

To reach Cliff Lake, keep left and after a couple of yards stay right where paths head left to Campbell Lake. Drop briefly, then rise to a view of Campbell Lake. Switchback just before the outlet stream from Cliff Lake and traverse to the other side of the ridge. Make two more short switchbacks and travel above the outlet along a rocky bench to Cliff Lake.

To make the loop, return to the junction of the trail to Summit Lake and turn west. Walk along the edge of a pond and descend to a meadow. Keep left at a junction and 50 feet farther pass a campsite where a sign points to Summit Lake. Travel on the level and climb through varied terrain then descend into a little inner valley of nice woods. Pass small Summit Meadow Lake and just beyond it come to Summit Lake.

To complete the loop, walk along the edge of the lake, cross the outlet and follow the route to the right to the junction of the trail to Marble Valley. Keep right and descend to a meadow and stream at the obscure junction of the path to Little Elk Lake and continue down to the junction with No. 11W21.

Trail Sign below Summit Lake

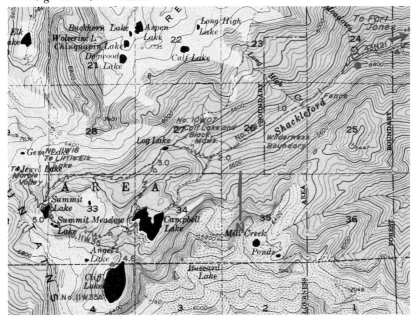

10 TANNERS PEAK

One day trip
Distance: 3.5 miles one way
Elevation gain: 3,890 feet
Allow 3½ to 4½ hours one way
Usually open June through October
High Point: 6,610 feet
Topographic map:
  U.S.G.S. Sawyers Bar, Calif.
  15'   1955

No Permit Required

The craggy summit of Tanners Peak, probably named for a miner who worked in this region around 1878, is reached by 3.5 miles of frequently steep trail. Present and past mining activity can be seen along the climb and the view from the top includes the wooded slopes of the Klamath National Forest and portions of the Marble Mountain Wilderness. Carry water if you make the hike from late summer through fall.

Drive on the road between Etna and Sawyers Bar to the entrance to Idlewild Campground, 19 miles southwest of Etna or 6.0 miles northeast of Sawyers Bar. The road is unpaved from 3.0 miles beyond Etna to 6.0 miles east of the campground entrance. Turn

north, keep left at a spur to the camp area and continue along 41N37 for 2.0 miles and park near the large sign marking the beginning of the Tanners Peak Trail, just before a bridge.

After climbing a few hundred yards meet an abandoned canal and turn right, following it for about 90 feet, then turn left and cross the canal. Climb very steeply for the next mile. An old metal marker embedded in a tree on the right side of the trail notes the 1.0 mile point, but it's easy to miss on the way up. A few feet beyond this marker the trail turns west and rises more moderately. A sign at 1.2 miles points downslope to water. About 0.2 mile farther pass the remains of a log building on the right that once was part of the Hennings Mine.

Continue in the woods until turning northwest and traverse up a rocky, brush covered slope. At the ridge face the trail turns left back into the woods and after a few yards another signed path heads down to water. A few hundred feet farther the trail turns sharply uphill at a tree with a 2.0 mile marker.

Climb steeply in tight switchbacks for a short distance then contour along a north facing slope. Come to more old mining remains at 2.7 miles. Pieces of weathered logs form an outline of one building and evidence of a stamp mill lies downslope. At one time, ore extracted from the One Hundred Dollar Mine near the summit was carried here by burros and put through the first stage of processing before being transported down the peak.

The trail climbs directly up from this site for a few feet then turns right and contours through woods and brush. From here until the summit ridge, look back frequently to familiarize yourself with the terrain. The trail becomes faint in a few places on the rocky slope and the more landmarks you can recall the less cross-country you'll have if you miss the route on the way back. Contour for several hundred yards then switchback up the slope. If you lose the trail, keep left of the cliffs and aim for the flat part of the ridge to the right of the summit block.

Turn left at the ridge crest and drop slightly on the southwest side. Walk along the rocky path until entering woods and coming to the first digging of the One Hundred Dollar Mine. The second digging is a few yards farther past a sign indicating water. The trail to the summit begins at the first digging and climbs to the north through woods before switchbacking to the top.

32

Tanners Peak from near Etna Summit

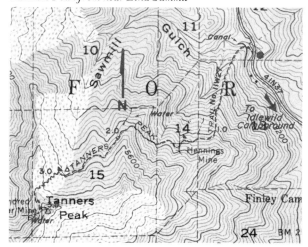

11 TAYLOR LAKE LOOP

One day trip or backpack
Distance: 4.7 miles round trip
Elevation gain: 1,750 feet round trip
Allow 3 hours round trip
Usually open June through October
High Point: 7,450 feet
Topographic map:
   U.S.G.S. Etna, Calif.
   15'   **1955**

No Permit Required

Taylor Lake, situated southeast of Etna Summit, is a popular destination in itself because of the easy hike in and the good fishing. But an even more scenic and interesting outing is possible by doing the trip as a 4.7 mile loop. (This mileage assumes you won't be driving a four-wheel drive vehicle. If you are, you can park at the beginning of the 0.6 mile trail proper to Taylor Lake and thereby save 1.8 miles of hiking.) A side trip west and south from Taylor Lake to Hogan Lake affords an additional opportunity for the more adventuresome to enjoy the region's complex terrain.

Proceed 10 miles southwest of the town of Etna to Etna Summit and then head downhill for 0.4 mile to a road on your left identified by a stop sign and a small marker stating Taylor Lake. The road from Etna is unpaved 3.0 miles southwest of the town. If approaching from the west, the turnoff is 15 miles northeast of Sawyers Bar. (Coming this way, you'll meet the unpaved surface 3.0 miles below the summit.) Turn onto the road to Taylor Lake and after about 0.3 mile stay left where the road forks. After another 0.3 mile keep right if you don't have a four-wheel drive vehicle, head downhill to the large, open area and park here. If you are able to drive to the trailhead (or are walking), continue on the main road for 0.9 mile, keeping straight where spurs head left and right, to a big switchback at the official trailhead for Taylor Lake. The steepest grade is just beyond the lower parking area: once past it you shouldn't have any problem.

From the trailhead, climb briefly and then travel through open, alpine-like terrain. Where you come to a fork take either branch and continue to the northeast end of the lake. A large camp area, frequented by pushy deer, is to the right near the north shore.

To visit Hogan Lake, follow the trail along the east shore and around to the southern tip. Begin climbing to the west and after about 1.0 mile curve south and descend for another 1.0 mile to the lake. The trail may be faint but the terrain is suitable for cross-country travel.

To make the recommended loop, follow the trail beside the east shore of Taylor Lake to about mid-length at a huge rock fire ring. Veer left and begin climbing. You're aiming for the obvious pass on the wall above you. Many use-paths join and diverge on the lower slope but as you gain elevation look for one primary route to the right (southeast) of the main gulley. The route is a bit rubbly occasionally but if you follow the correct alignment you'll never be on difficult or dangerous terrain. Come to the crest where you'll have a view over farmland and hills to Mt. Shasta (see No. 40) and meet the Pacific Crest Trail. The section that heads south passes below Bingham Lake (No. 13) after about 7.0 miles.

Turn left, traverse uphill and continue climbing in two switchbacks. If you want to visit Smith Lake — where there's no camping because of the rocky shoreline — begin the cross-country descent from the first switchback. Traverse high along the basin wall above Smith Lake. You can see the jagged crest of Castle Crags (No. 41) on the southern horizon.

Reenter woods, have the first view northwest to the Marble Mountains and begin descending through increasingly open terrain. Switchback twice and look ahead and below for a section of the road you'll soon be joining. Continue downhill for a short distance to where you're in line with a saddle above you on the crest. Turn left, leaving the trail, descend for an easy 300 yards to the road, turn left again and follow it for 0.5 mile to the switchback at the Taylor Lake trailhead.

34

Fisherman at Taylor Lake

12 GRIZZLY LAKE

One day trip or backpack
Distance: 6 miles one way
Elevation gain: 3,880 feet; loss 1,140 feet
Allow 4½ to 6 hours one way
Usually open July through mid-October
High Point: 7,100 feet
Topographic map:
U.S.G.S. Cecilville, Calif.
15'   1955

Permit Required

Some wag once suggested that Grizzly Lake was so named because it's a bear to reach. More accurate, perhaps, is the fact that California, like much of the West, once had a large population of grizzlies. But the last known grizzly in the state was shot in the Sierra during the mid-1920's. In addition to considerable climbing and descending on the way in (which means that this loss has to be regained on the trip back), there's only a use-trail for the final mile between Grizzly Meadows and the lake. Of course, this hard work is rewarded with superlative scenery: Grizzly Lake is surrounded on three sides by a two-mile long glacier that sprawls across the northern slopes of Thompson Peak, at 9,002 feet the highest point in the Trinity Alps. The lake's outlet creek is a spectacular several hundred foot high waterfall.

On FH 93 drive 27 miles west from Callahan or 2.5 miles east of Cecilville to a sign marking the road to East Fork Campground. (Trail No's. 13 through 17 also are reached by FH 93.) Turn south onto paved 37N24, cross a bridge and 3.0 miles farther cross a second span. Along this stretch you'll eventually be able to see south to Thompson Peak. A few hundred yards beyond the second bridge keep right on unpaved 37N02 (that may be signed 37N07), following the sign to Grizzly Lake. After about 0.2 mile continue straight then 3.0 miles farther curve right, following the sign to China Gulch Trail, and after a few feet pass through a deep cut. Less than a mile farther, bear right, keeping the canyon on your right. In slightly over a mile don't complete the switchback but continue straight ahead. A canyon now will be on your left. Continue 1.0 mile to China Creek and 0.2 mile farther come to the signed trailhead.

Climb steadily and steeply through deep woods for 1.0 mile to a level, forested saddle. Keep right and descend through open, more arid woods for another 1.0 mile to the junction of the trail to Grizzly Creek and Hobo Gulch. A refreshing creek is a few hundred feet down the trail to the right.

To continue the hike, turn left (east) at the junction, following the sign to Grizzly Lake. Climb through timber then contour along the steep rocky slope above Lower Grizzly Meadows. Pass through several sequences of deep woods and small clearings before coming to upper Grizzly Meadows.

The official trail ends just beyond the campsite at the south end of the meadow. A path continues through woods to a boulder field that extends for 0.5 mile to the head of the valley. If snow is still on the ground be careful not to step into moats around the edges of the rocks. Hike up the rocky floor for about 0.3 mile from the camp then watch for a faint path rising up the valley wall on your left. This tread is in a small gully just beyond a mass of downward sloping slabs and the route is difficult to spot until you're a little past it. Although steep, the path is up a staircase of small rocks and/or grass clumps. If you find yourself on solid rock, you've taken the wrong route!

Where you reach the top of this pitch, veer slightly left and continue climbing steeply. From here until the lake it's very important to keep looking back and noting reference points so you'll return by the same route. Continue climbing and then begin curving right. The route doesn't go all the way to the ridge top but instead becomes less steep and contours in a southerly direction. Continue across the grass, brush and rock covered slope to a fringe of trees and climb slightly before reaching the outlet falls and lake.

Grizzly Lake

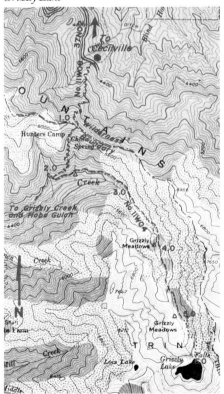

13 BINGHAM LAKE

One day trip or backpack
Distance: 4.5 miles one way
Elevation gain: 2,350 feet; loss 300 feet
Allow 3 to 3½ hours one way
Usually open June through October
High Point: 7,300 feet
Topographic maps:
U.S.G.S. Coffee Creek, Calif.
15'   1955
U.S.G.S. Etna, Calif.
15'   1955

No Permit Required

Hiking to Bingham Lake is like traveling over an immense jigsaw puzzle where all the pieces fit perfectly but each seems to be from a completely different scene. You'll climb through woods to immense open grassy slopes and then traverse high on a sheer rock wall before making the 0.2 mile cross-country climb to sawtooth ridge rimmed Bingham Lake.

Proceed on paved FH 93 for 16 miles west of Callahan or 14 miles east of Cecilville to narrow, unpaved Road 10W19 that angles off the north side of the highway about 100 yards east of the entrance to Trail Creek Campground. Road 10W19 is steep for the first several yards but has a moderate to gradual grade for the remaining 0.3 mile to a stream. Park off the road just before the flow.

Ford the shallow stream, walk several yards through a flat, open area then veer up to the right onto a rough road. Where it forks keep left, make an S curve and continue uphill beneath the mix of pine, cedar and other frequently large conifers. At 1.0 mile drop slightly then resume rising for 0.4 mile to the end of the road. Continue up in the same direction you were heading for about 100 feet to the top of a large camp area. Look right for a blaze, follow a trail down to the stream and ford it.

Traverse east up the bank along a trail and then wind up through woods, that thin as you gain elevation, for 0.5 mile to a road and a cabin. More remains of past mining activity are farther west down this road. Turn right (east) and follow the road uphill. After you leave the woods you'll be able to see south to Thompson Peak (refer to No. 12). Continue traversing the grassy, treeless slope to a possibly unsigned trail angling back on your left, the Pacific Crest Trail No. 2000, and turn onto it. (If you followed the section of the PCT that heads downhill here for 3.0 miles you'd come to the trailhead for hike No's. 16 and 17.)

Traverse up to a second road, cross it and resume traveling along a trail. Switchback twice and come to a crest where you'll be able to see Mt. Shasta (refer to No. 40) and Mt. Eddy (see No. 18) and directly down onto Jackson Lake. From this crest curve sharply left and traverse along a rocky slope. Enter woods and descend gradually to a small saddle. Curve left, switchback down once then climb and traverse upward along a face of white rock high above the head of a large valley. You may hear bells and lowing from cattle grazing below.

Again reenter woods and mostly traverse down the valley wall. About 0.5 mile beyond the cliff face come to an apparent low point along the trail and on the ridge crest above. At this spot there are almost no trees ahead and a large, obvious gully of rocks crosses the trail. A stake also may mark this point. If you continued along No. 2000 for about another 7.0 miles you'd meet the path up from Taylor Lake (No. 11).

Turn right, leaving the trail, and work your way up the light colored rubble, staying right (south) of the gully proper. Contour to the left (north) across a little basin of boulders then have easier going for the final 150 yards as you follow a vegetated swale to the lake shore. Turn right and cross the outlet to reach rock outcroppings that provide a good place to enjoy lunch and the scenery.

Old mine ruins

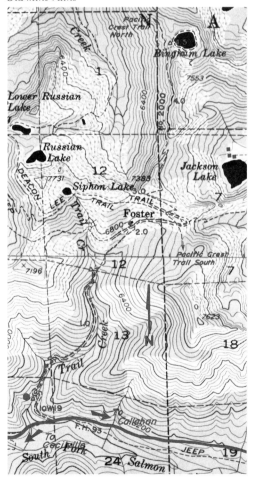

14 FISH and TWIN LAKES

One day trip
Distance: 1.8 miles to Fish Lake;
   0.9 mile one way additional to Twin Lakes
Elevation gain: 980 feet to Fish Lake;
   720 feet additional to Twin Lakes
Allow 1 hour one way to Fish Lake; 45 minutes
   one way additional to Twin Lakes
Usually open June through October
High Point: 6,400 feet
Topographic map:
   U.S.G.S. Coffee Creek, Calif.
   15'   **1955**

No Permit Required

The two pronged trip to Fish and Twin Lakes is a perfect choice when you don't want to work *too* hard for your scenic rewards. Of particular note are the open areas you pass through on both forks of the outing. Fish and Twin Lakes are in the next vally to the west from Trail Gulch Lake (No. 15) and, in fact, a 1.5 mile connector joins the two basins. These two valleys are as different in appearance as Fish and Twin Lakes are from each other. Since grazing is allowed in the area and the cattle seem partial to shorelines, this isn't a good choice for a backpack. Similarly, begin the hike with a full water bottle as sources along the hike probably are contaminated.

Drive on FH 93 for 16 miles west of Callahan or 14 miles east of Cecilville to a sign marking the road to Trail Creek Campground. The access road to Bingham Lake (No. 13) begins just east of this sign and access to hike No's. 12, 16 and 17 also is from FH 93. Turn south, drive downhill, keep left at the campground entrance and 0.4 mile farther

come to a junction. Keep right on 39N05, as indicated by the sign, and after 0.1 mile cross the East Fork of the South Fork. After another 0.4 mile keep left on the main road at a spur, several yards farther stay right and continue the final 0.8 mile to a sign on your right identifying the Fish Lake Trail and listing mileages.

The trail begins across 39N05 from the sign and follows up along an old skid road. The surrounding woods are grubby at first but they soon become their usual attractive selves. After 0.2 mile begin traveling along a trail proper and parallel Fish Creek. Eventually cross it, climb at an erratic grade for 0.3 mile and then reford the flow. Continue up in woods to the edge of a treeless area of bushes and grass. About 30 yards into the clearing look right for a path, that may not be signed, heading down through grass to Fish Creek. This is the route to Twin Lakes.

To complete the hike to Fish Lake, stay left and climb gradually through the semi-open area of grass, bushes, false hellebore and a few uncommonly immense deciduous trees. Cross a ribbon of rock rubble and traverse more steeply up a slope of conifers and lush ferns to the signed junction of the connector to the routes to Trail Gulch Lake and over South Fork Divide (No. 27). To reach Fish Lake turn right and walk 150 yards to the grass-rimmed shore.

To visit Twin Lakes, retrace your route to the possibly unsigned junction in the clearing at 1.1 miles. Walk down to the stream, cross it and a short distance farther cross a smaller flow. Begin winding up through an attractive coniferous woods. Traverse, curve into a side valley, cross the outlet stream from Twin Lakes and continue uphill a short distance to a large open swath.

Climb in the same direction you were heading, at first traveling parallel to a deeply rutted trail and then following occasional blazes and cairns. Stay near the left (south) side of the clearing and about 200 yards from where the woods resume at the top end be looking for a sign on a log on the ground pointing right to the obscure route to I-Am-Up Ridge and left to Twin Lakes.

Veer left and walk across a little clearing of grass and scattered small rocks to an obvious tread that begins at the edge of the woods. After several yards turn left at a junction and rise 200 yards through woods to the grassy area around the lake. Cross the outlet and veer right for several yards to the shore.

Hiker at Twin Lakes

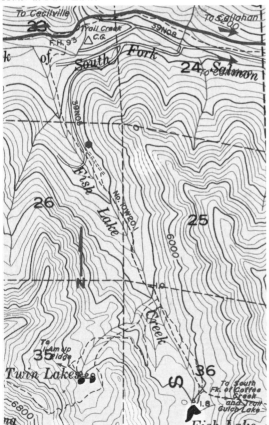

15 TRAIL and LONG GULCH LAKES LOOP

One day trip or backpack
Distance: 7 miles round trip
Elevation gain: 2,265 feet
Allow 4½ to 6 hours round trip
Usually open late June through October
High Point: 7,545 feet
Topographic map:
    U.S.G.S. Coffee Creek, Calif.
    15'   **1955**

No Permit Required

Although one-half of the loop past Trail and Long Gulch Lakes is along old dirt roads, these marks of man don't intrude unduly into the enjoyment of the woods, meadows, lakes and open ridges. You have the option of several side trips. From the junction just west of Trail Gulch Lake you can visit Fish Lake (No. 14) or climb over South Fork Divide (No. 27). From above Long Gulch Lake you could head south to the North Fork of Coffee Creek. Since grazing is permitted throughout the area, begin the hike with fresh water and carry a purifying chemical if you're backpacking.

Coming from the east, proceed from Callahan on FH 93, the paved road that connects this community with Cecilville, for 13 miles to just beyond a summit where a short spur heads left to the beginning of hike No's. 16 and 17. Continue on FH 93 another 0.5 mile to the next road left. It angles off sharply from the highway and is marked with a stop sign. Turn onto the unpaved surface, after 1.3 miles pass the trailhead for Long Gulch Lake and continue another 0.9 mile to the signed start of the route to Trail Gulch Lake. Approaching from the west, drive on FH 93 about 14 miles east of Cecilville to a sign marking the road to Trail Creek Camp-

ground. Turn here, keep left at the campground entrance, stay left again a short distance farther and follow 39N08 for about 2.0 miles to the Trail Gulch Lake trailhead.

Hike along the abandoned roadbed through deep woods and across lush clearings for 2.7 miles. A few hundred yards beyond a fence where the road curves down to the left keep straight on a trail and rise gradually along a rocky slope. Reenter woods and come to the first junction. You'll need a wilderness permit to continue south of South Fork Divide. Turn left and drop slightly for 0.3 mile to the wooded north shore of the lake.

To make the loop, continue along the trail to the marshy area east of the lake. A well-worn path starts across the exit creek directly east of a campsite. Follow this trail for several hundred feet then turn slightly left. Climb gradually along a grassy slope, heading for the northernmost (left) clump of bushes below the rock rim. A faint trail begins in the woods a few feet below the bushes and after several yards turns right and switchbacks steeply up to a pass. To continue along a trail, keep right and descend to the junction of the trail to the North Fork of Coffee Creek, that also is in a Wilderness. Turn left and climb to Trail Gulch Divide on the crest above Long Gulch Lake.

To travel cross-country from the pass at 4.0 miles turn left and follow along the open ridge crest to a fine overlook at its highest point. Descend gradually along the crest and where the vegetation becomes dense drop slightly to the right and continue in an easterly direction along an animal trail. Below outcroppings take a high trail through bushes to another viewpoint. Scramble down a short pitch and cross the wooded saddle to its eastern end and meet the official trail at a sign reading *Trail Gulch Divide*.

From the divide descend through woods for 0.6 mile to the spur to the lake. Turn left and climb slightly for 0.2 mile and then travel near the north shore. You can eliminate this backtracking to the lake by heading cross-country from the main trail at the 5.0 mile point.

To complete the loop, continue gradually downhill along the main trail. Near 6.0 miles cross several creeks and a large meadow then reenter woods, cross Long Gulch Creek and travel the last 0.7 mile along an old logging road. If you haven't arranged a shuttle, turn left and walk along 39N08 for 0.9 mile to your car.

Trail Gulch Lake

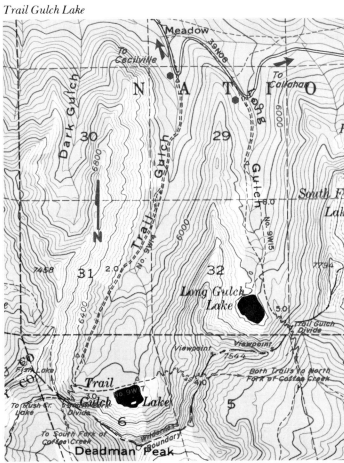

16 HIDDEN LAKE

One-half day trip
Distance: 1.0 mile one way
Elevation gain: 500 feet
Allow ½ hour one way
Usually open June through October
High Point: 6,650 feet
Topographic map:
  U.S.G.S. Coffee Creek, Calif.
  15'   1955

Permit Required

The trail to Hidden Lake tucked, appropriately, at the base of a steep-walled cirque is the shortest in this guide. If your muscles are only beginning to warm up by the time you return you can head south several yards before you reach the starting point and make the 2.3 mile hike to South Fork Lakes (No. 17) or follow the Pacific Crest Trail as far as you're inclined.

Drive on FH 93 for 13 miles southwest of Callahan or 17 miles northeast of Cecilville to just west of the summit where a small sign marks the route of the Pacific Crest Trail. The road to the parking area for the trail at Carter Meadows Viewpoint begins from the south side of the pavement and is identified by a stop sign. Hike No's. 12 through 15 begin farther west along FH 93.

The trail proper starts midway between FH 93 and the parking area but paths also shortcut down to the main route from the large bulletin board near the end of the spur. Descend for about 50 feet from the parking area to the junction of the trail to South Fork Lakes. Keep right and follow an erratic grade of ups and downs through attractive woods and open slopes. You'll have views south to dramatic rock pinnacles and down into the huge valley that collects the headwaters of the South Fork of the Scott River. Come to a treeless crest, continue up in deeper woods and then drop briefly to the shore of the forest-rimmed lake. A good campsite will be found on the northwestern shore.

Hidden Lake

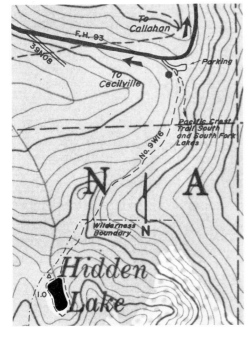

17 SOUTH FORK LAKES

One day trip or backpack
Distance: 2.3 miles one way
Elevation gain: 870 feet; loss 320 feet
Allow 1½ to 2 hours one way
Usually open June through mid-October
High Point: 6,750 feet
Topographic map:
  U.S.G.S. Coffee Creek, Calif.
  15'   **1955**

Permit Required

The delightful hike to the South Fork Lakes travels through and past scenic terrain that is remarkably varied, considering the relatively short length of the trail. Meadows, big and small, massive rock outcroppings, two lakes and various types of coniferous forests are a few of the visual treats. Even the grade alternates from gradual to stretches of muscle-stretching steep. You could combine the trip with the even shorter hike to Hidden Lake

(No. 16) that begins from the same trailhead or continue for as long as you have time or energy along the Pacific Crest Trail from the junction at 1.2 miles.

Proceed on FH 93 for 13 miles southwest of Callahan or 17 miles northeast of Cecilville to just west of a crest where a small sign marks the route of the Pacific Crest Trail. A short spur road to Carter Meadows Viewpoint and parking for the South Fork and Hidden Lakes trails begins from the south side of FH 93 and is identified by a stop sign. Hike No's. 12 through 15 begin farther west along FH 93.

The trail starts midway between FH 93 and the parking area but paths also shortcut down to the main route from the large bulletin board near the end of the spur. Descend for about 50 feet from the parking area to the junction of the 1.0 mile trail to Hidden Lake. Keep left and traverse down along the wooded slope forming the west wall at the head of the huge valley that collects the first drainage for the South Fork of the Scott River.

Pass through a section of more open terrain as you travel along the base of massive rock outcroppings. Reenter woods and follow an erratic, but mostly downhill, grade. Cross a small stream, several yards farther ford the outlet from South Fork Lakes and 250 yards beyond it come to the signed junction of the route to South Fork Lakes. The Pacific Crest Trail traverses north from here.

Turn right and wind uphill for 0.2 mile to the edge of a large, grassy bowl. Follow the faint tread down through the clearing to a fire ring at the edge of a rocky area that borders the south end of the meadow. Continue in the same direction you were heading for a few more feet and then bear right and pick up the once again obvious tread. Cross a rocky stream bed that is dry by late summer, or sooner, and traverse to the north. Begin climbing, soon at a very steep angle. Have a respite as you contour through a boggy area on the slope and then resume winding steeply uphill.

Eventually, come to the edge of the basin holding the South Fork Lakes. Cross an open, grassy area, reenter woods and walk gradually uphill to the first and smaller of the two lakes. To reach the second, follow along the northwest shore to where the trail stops. Bear slightly right and walk cross-country for 200 yards through woods with little ground cover to the north shore of the upper lake.

Trail Sign

47

18 DEADFALL LAKES

One day trip or backpack
Distance: 3 miles one way
Elevation gain: 1,700 feet
Allow 1½ hours one way
Usually open late June through October
High Point: 8,100 feet
Topographic maps:
    U.S.G.S. China Mountain, Calif.
    15'   1955
    U.S.G.S. Weed, Calif.
    15'   1954

No Permit Required

Although short, the absolutely delightful hike past Deadfall Lakes to the ridge above offers an impressive number of special treats: around the third week in June a charming assortment of wildflowers plus one very exotic variety line sections of the route; the view at the crest is engrossingly far-ranging and for a face-to-face look at Mt. Shasta 16 air miles away you can make a relatively easy 0.6 mile, 1,100 foot cross-country climb to the summit of Mt. Eddy; and unique to most high country outings, you have the opportunity of a comfortable swim in one of the small upper lakes.

You can reach Road 42N17 that passes the trailhead either from I-5 or California 3. For the former, follow I-5 4.0 miles north of Weed or 24 miles south of Yreka to the signed exit to Stewart Springs Road and Edgewood. Turn west, and after several yards at a T-junction turn right, following the sign to Stewart Springs Road. After a short distance turn left, following a similar sign. At about 4.0 miles turn right onto unpaved 42N17, as indicated by the sign pointing to Deadfall Meadow. Follow 42N17 for 11 miles to a switchback to the right and a sign identifying Deadfall Meadow on the left shoulder and park in the signed area across the road. If you're approaching from California 3, follow it 16 miles south of Callahan or 20 miles north of Trinity Center to signed 42N17 at the north end of a bridge over Blue Creek. Turn northeast and follow unpaved 42N17 12 miles to the switchback at Deadfall Meadow.

Walk into the meadow, cross several small streams a short distance before Deadfall Creek and then after fording the latter turn left and begin heading up the valley. Again have easy crossings of a small stream and then Deadfall Creek and continue up through a meadow that supports a large population of marsh marigolds, wallflowers, larkspurs, shooting stars, columbines, buttercups and forget-me-nots. Where you make a short traverse across a squishy area look for pitcher plants (also called cobra plant, because of its hooded shape, and Darlingtonia). These carnivorous plants are infrequently seen and, although not pretty, certainly are interesting. Remember *never* to pick any wildflowers — leave them for the enjoyment of hikers who follow.

Rise gradually along a section of old road, cross Deadfall Creek for the third time and about 75 feet farther come to a fork. To visit the largest and/or lowest of the Deadfall Lakes keep right.

To complete the hike to the upper lakes and the crest, stay left, rise more noticeably and soon have a view of the largest of the Deadfall Lakes. Continue up along a trail and just beyond a switchback skirt a tarn that should make for good swimming. Wind up over attractive, sparsely wooded, rocky terrain for a short distance to a larger tarn where the trail becomes faint. Do not cross the inlet stream but instead parallel it up to a little meadowy area. Veer right, look for a well-defined tread traversing up to the southwest and follow it to the crest.

You'll have an overview of the Deadfall Lakes basin and you'll be able to see south to Castle Crags (No. 41) and Mt. Lassen and southwest to high points in the Trinity Alps. To reach the summit of Mt. Eddy turn east or for an easier side trip you can head southwest along the ridge top. As is obvious from the crest, cross-country travel in the Deadfall Lakes basin isn't difficult so you could roam throughout it.

Upper and Lower Deadfall Lakes

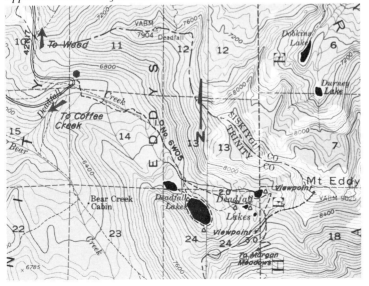

19 BIG BEAR LAKE

One day trip or backpack
Distance: 4 miles one way
Elevation gain: 2,800 feet
Allow 2½ hours one way
Usually open June through October
High Point: 5,800 feet
Topographic map:
   U.S.G.S. Bonanza King, Calif.
   15'   1955

Permit Required

The pleasant hike to Big Bear Lake has, in miniature, many of the features that make the Trinities so appealing: a respectably sized lake, variation in vegetation from oaks to tall conifers, an expansive setting and, paradoxically, high rock walls. Although you won't have the pleasure of traveling through huge, lush meadows that grace so many hikes, the variety of wildflowers will compensate somewhat for this deficiency. Also, unlike many trails in the Trinities — and also the Marbles — there isn't access to a network of other routes. But in a way that can be a good point because, for a change, you won't be frustrated by all those trails not taken.

Approaching from the south, drive on California 3 a bit over 15 miles north of Trinity Center (that is 28 miles north of Weaverville) to an unmarked road on your left (west) a short distance beyond a mileage sign (facing north) and a private sign for Bonanza King. Turn west and follow the road 1.0 mile to a sign on the left identifying the beginning of the Bear Lake Trail 7W03 just before a bridge over Bear Creek. Coming from the north, take California 3 south from Callahan for about 17 miles to unidentified Sunflower Flat, a large, openish area with a few buildings off the right (west) side of the highway. Turn right onto an unsigned road here and follow it south for 2.0 miles to the signed trailhead just beyond the bridge over Bear Creek. Be assured that locating the start of the hike is the only route-finding problem of the trip.

Traverse above Bear Creek at an erratic grade for 0.9 mile and cross it on a bridge. Begin winding uphill, still at an irregular grade with even a short descent farther on. Early in the season you'll be able to enjoy the dogwood blooms. This tree, inconspicuous in summer, is among the most obvious in late spring with its big, creamy flowers and in autumn when its otherwise unnoteworthy leaves turn a showy, peach-hued red. Other wildflowers you'll enjoy farther along the hike include deer brush, tiger lilies, columbines, forget-me-nots, heather, buttercups, spirea and larkspur.

Curve gradually left on a rocky tread and once again travel near Bear Creek through woods that have become mostly coniferous. The trail surface is smoother as it follows a gentle grade through deeper woods where ferns add further lushness to the setting. Eventually, leave the forest and begin climbing along a more open slope of pines, manzanita and rocks. Make a set of switchbacks in woods and cross through a brushy area where, if you make the hike around the end of June, you will be treated to the rich scent of azaleas. Unlike its non-fragrant relative, the rhododendron, one azalea bush can perfume the surrounding air for hundreds of feet.

Again come to an open slope of rock slabs. Turn around for a good view of Mt. Shasta (see No. 40) and Mt. Eddy (see No. 18) to the west of Mt. Shasta. Climb a bit more, cross the outlet and a couple of hundred feet farther come to the lake's shore. Campsites are plentiful.

Big Bear Lake

20 CARIBOU LAKES

One day trip or backpack
Distance: 8.5 miles one way
Elevation gain: 2,400 feet; loss 540 feet
Allow 5 to 6 hours one way
Usually open July through October
High Point: 7,200 feet
Topographic map:
  U.S.G.S. Coffee Creek, Calif.
  15'   1955

Permit Required

Eleven trails in this guide (No's. 20 through 30) begin from Coffee Creek Road. Each one of these routes has its own distinctive personality — by no means have you viewed all the scenery if you've hiked only one or two. The trip into the Caribou Lakes basin is the most popular, particularly for backpackers, of all the trails from Coffee Creek Road, probably because of the superlative scenery. Certainly the setting is among the most impressive in the Trinity Alps but, because of this heavy use, the area is not as remote as the distance in would indicate.

An interesting loop requiring 900 extra feet of uphill is possible by following the abandoned trail that climbs over Peak 8118 (No. 21) between Caribou Meadows at 3.5 miles and rejoins the main route at 7.1 miles just above Snowslide Lake. For a longer trek you could follow ill-defined trails south to the Stewart Fork (see No. 33) or northwest to the Salmon River drainage. Because of past improper camping techniques in the Caribou Lakes basin, the water may be contaminated so use a purification method if you're camping or carry an adequate supply of water for a day hike.

Drive on California 3 for 36 miles north of Weaverville or 27 miles south of Callahan to the community of Coffee Creek. Turn west and in a short distance keep straight on Coffee Creek Road. After 4.5 miles the pavement ends and although never steep, the Coffee Creek Road occasionally is narrow and rough beyond here. Keep left at a fork about 14 miles beyond the end of the pavement and continue approximately 1.0 mile farther to the spur down to Big Flat Campground. Turn right and drive 100 feet to the trailhead parking.

Head south from the signed trailhead along an old roadbed then curve right and follow a trail down to the crossing of the Salmon River. Packing a pair of tennis shoes to wear while making the possible ford would keep your boots dry. Traverse up the bank to a level, semi-open area, cross it and begin climbing in nine gentle switchbacks. During the climb you'll have views of Mountain Meadow Ranch and across the valley to a section of the trail to the Yellow Rose Mine (No. 24) and the pass above Ward Lake (No. 23) plus occasional glimpses of Caribou Mountain.

Reenter woods, pass through a small open area then make two long traverses separated by a switchback to a saddle at 3.5 miles where a sign identifies the open slopes as Caribou Meadows. Contour across the grassy slope on the north side of the ridge then reenter woods and begin climbing gradually. Near 4.0 miles the trail has been blasted out of massive granite slabs. The exit creek from Little Caribou Lake cascades down the center of this exposed rock. Again reenter woods and after 1.0 mile cross a small stream at the edge of the lush green swath of Browns Meadow. Switchback up through woods to a saddle then traverse gradually up along a tree dotted slope.

Beyond 6.0 miles you can look south to the cirque that is your destination. As you travel farther along the steep rock wall that forms the head of the valley holding Caribou Creek you'll eventually be able to see Lower Caribou Lake and a portion of Caribou Lake. Jagged peaks that form the heart of the Trinity Alps fill the horizon to the southwest. The old alignment of the trail meets the newer route just before a series of switchbacks down to Snowslide Lake. Beyond it climb gradually along granite slabs and then wind on the level for 0.3 mile through a fantastic maze of large, rounded boulders, deep pools and, in early summer, sprays of delicate pink flowers to the north shore of Caribou Lake.

Thunderhead over Caribou Lake

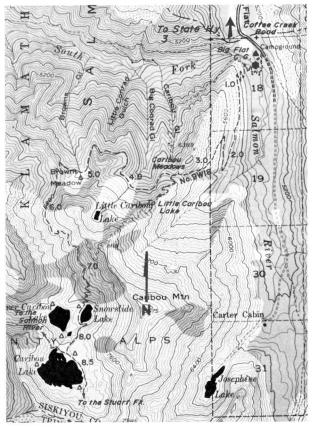

21 LITTLE CARIBOU LAKE and PEAK 8118

One day trip
Distance: 5 miles one way to Little Caribou
  Lake; 0.6 mile additional one way to
  Viewpoint
Elevation gain: 2,250 feet to Little Caribou
  Lake; 815 feet additional to Viewpoint
Allow 2 to 2½ hours one way to Little Caribou
  Lake; ½ hour additional one way to Viewpoint
Usually open late June through mid-October
High Point: 8,118 feet
Topographic map:
  U.S.G.S. Coffee Creek, Calif.
  15'   1955

Permit Required

Little Caribou Lake, tucked against the north side of Caribou Mountain, is visually unrelated to its considerably larger namesakes on the other side of the peak as you'll see from the viewpoint at Peak 8118 with its stunning overview of the Caribou Lakes basin (No. 20) and the rugged peaks beyond. A path continues down from the viewpoint to near the basin so you could make a loop and rejoin the trail you followed in at 3.5 miles. Because of a possible ford at the start of the hike, you may want to pack a pair of tennis shoes. Carry drinking water.

Proceed on California 3 for 36 miles north of Weaverville or 27 miles south of Callahan to the community of Coffee Creek. Turn west and in a short distance keep straight on Coffee Creek Road. After 4.5 miles the pavement ends and although never steep, Coffee Creek Road occasionally is narrow and rough beyond here. Pass the trailheads for hike No's. 25 through 30 and at a fork about 14 miles beyond the end of the pavement keep

left and continue approximately 1.0 mile farther to the spur down to Big Flat Campground. Turn right and drive 100 feet to trailhead parking. Hikes 21 through 24 also begin here.

Head south from the signed trailhead along an old roadbed then curve right and follow a trail down to the crossing of the Salmon River. Traverse up the opposite bank to a level, semi-open area, cross it and begin climbing in nine gentle switchbacks. As you traverse south along a slope of manzanita you can see across the Salmon River Valley to a section of the trail to the Yellow Rose and LeRoy Mines (No. 24) and the pass above Ward Lake (No. 23). The pinnacle of granite to the south has unofficially been dubbed the Little Matterhorn and you'll have occasional glimpses ahead to massive Caribou Mountain.

Reenter woods, pass through a small open area then make two long traverses separated by a switchback to a saddle at 3.5 miles where a sign identifies the open slopes as Caribou Meadows. Look for an unmarked path that angles up at about 40 degrees to the left from the main trail and take it. The tread is rough but easy to follow. Climb in many short switchbacks to an open spot with a view of Caribou Mountain. The trail eventually goes over the wooded point ahead to the right. Drop through a rocky area to a saddle with a view north to Packers Peak (No. 25).

Cross the remainder of the saddle, pass a digging and resume climbing. Switchback three times, make a long traverse to the west then wind up in seven more turns. At the last one where you can see an area of boulders and granite slabs, leave the trail and contour cross-country for 0.3 mile to Little Caribou Lake. Although you will have some sections of steep side-hilling and boulder hopping, the traverse is not difficult.

To visit the viewpoint, continue climbing through woods along the main trail from the above noted seventh switchback. The tread improves as you gain elevation. Go onto the northeast side of the slope and come to the viewpoint. In addition to the bird's-eye view over the Caribou Lakes basin, you can see Sawtooth Ridge (No. 22) to the south. The valley beyond Sawtooth Ridge holds Emerald and Sapphire Lakes (No. 33) and the high-point on the massive ridge to the west beyond the Caribou Lakes is Thompson Peak (see No. 12). From the crest, an abandoned trail — the former route to Caribou Lakes — winds down for 1.2 miles to No. 9W18.

The Caribou Lakes from Peak 8118

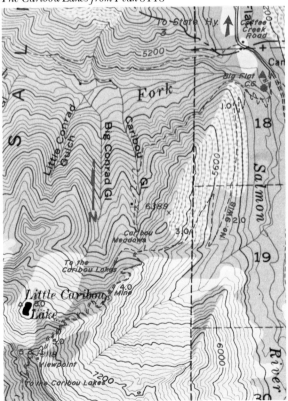

22 SAWTOOTH RIDGE

One day trip
Distance: 6.3 miles one way
Elevation gain: 2,595 feet
Allow 4 to 5 hours one way
Usually open July through October
High Point: 7,642 feet
Topographic maps:
    U.S.G.S. Coffee Creek, Calif.
    15'   **1955**
    U.S.G.S. Trinity Lake, Calif.
    15'   **1950**

Permit Required

If the 11 trails that begin from Coffee Creek Road (No's. 20 through 30) were listed in order of their scenic merits, the one to Sawtooth Ridge would be near — if not at — the head of the rankings. The middle portion is through an exceptionally attractive valley and the last 0.3 mile is up a unique open slope to a rocky crest that affords an impressive panorama.

Drive on California 3 for 36 miles north of Weaverville or 27 miles south of Callahan to the community of Coffee Creek. Turn west and in a short distance keep straight on Coffee Creek Road. After 4.5 miles the pavement ends and although never steep, the road occasionally is narrow and rough beyond here. Keep left at a fork about 14 miles beyond the end of the pavement and continue approximately 1.0 mile more to the spur down to Big Flat Campground. (As of early 1981, public vehicular travel along Coffee Creek Road beyond here was not permitted. However, this management policy may change, so you might want to check at the Coffee Creek Ranger Station beforehand to learn if parking is possible at the trailhead.) Turn right and drive 100 feet to parking spaces.

Retrace your route back up to Coffee Creek Road, turn right and continue along the scenic road, past a locked gate, for a total of 2.3 miles from the parking area to a sign identifying the trail to Kidd Creek, Ward Lake and Swift Creek. Turn left onto the trail and climb through woods at a gradual grade except for one short set of steep switchbacks. At an unmarked fork keep left and 0.7 mile from the road come to the signed junction of the trail to Ward Lake.

Keep right, following the sign to Sawtooth Ridge, and after 150 feet cross Kidd Creek. One hundred yards beyond the stream come to a road and turn left. Where you come to another road turn left again and begin climbing. At a crest just beyond a grassy area where you reenter woods but several yards before the road ends veer right onto a trail and traverse down to the edge of a meadow. NOTE: the abandoned trail that covered the distance now done along roads between 3.2 and 4.2 miles may be reopened. So, if a sign and tread so indicate, continue on a trail beyond the ford of Kidd Creek. The alignment will be east of the road and travel above the latter's end for a short distance then drop to the meadow and rejoin the former trail at about the 4.4 mile point.

Walk along the valley floor that is exquisitely decorated with a pleasing balance of rocks, grass, scattered trees and other vegetation. On the right a stream tumbles down a rugged little gorge. At a faint fork keep left, several yards farther cross a small stream and immediately begin climbing, occasionally steeply, on a rocky tread. Level off briefly, descend steeply for a short distance to a stream crossing and then resume climbing to a rocky bench. Rise very steeply up the wooded slope in 13 switchbacks to the crest of the ridge. Traverse west along the nose of the ridge for several hundred feet until you begin traveling along the base of a lushy vegetated, treeless slope. Turn right, leaving the trail that continues down to Deer Creek (see No. 32) and travel cross-country up the pasture, called Horse Heaven, to the rocky crest.

You can peer west directly down for 4,000 feet onto Morris Meadows and Emerald Lake (No. 33). Sawtooth Mountain is on the other (west) wall of the valley of the Stuart Fork and on the other side of that ridge is Canyon Creek Lakes (No. 36). You can see south as far as the Yolla Bolla and closer to the south are Gibson Peak and lookout topped Granite Peak, a section of the trail from Granite Lake (No. 31) to the Deer Creek Valley and also a stretch of the Deer Creek Trail crossing a grassy portion of the valley floor directly below. The top of Caribou Mountain (see No. 21) is barely visible to the north.

Sawtooth Mountain from Sawtooth Ridge

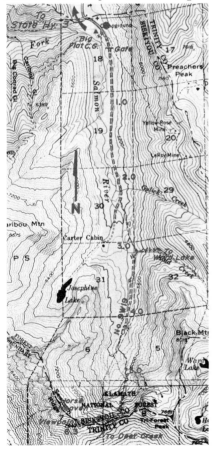

23 WARD LAKE

One day trip or backpack
Distance: 6.4 miles one way
Elevation gain: 2,500 feet; loss 450 feet
Allow 4 to 4½ hours one way
Usually open July through October
High Point: 7,550 feet
Topographic map:
U.S.G.S. Coffee Creek, Calif.
15'   1955

Permit Required

The combination of rugged peaks, sprawling meadows and lakes comprising the scene along the majority of hikes in the Trinity and Marble Mountains are all present, although on a slightly less imposing scale, on the hike to Ward Lake. After a pleasant road walk, the trail travels through woods to a long, open valley and winds up its rocky, convoluted head to a pass that affords extensive views before descending to the lake. You can extend the hike for another 1.2 miles to Horseshoe Lake or even farther by continuing east to the Swift Creek Trail and from there heading north to the route to Union Lake (No. 28) or south to the one to Granite Lake (No. 31), to cite only two possibilities.

Proceed on California 3 for 36 miles north of Weaverville or 27 miles south of Callahan to the community of Coffee Creek. Turn west and in a short distance keep straight on Coffee Creek Road. After 4.5 miles the pavement ends and although never steep, the Coffee Creek Road occasionally is narrow and rough beyond here. Pass the trailheads for hike No's. 25 through 30, keep left at a fork about 14 miles beyond the end of the pavement and

continue approximately 1.0 mile farther to the spur down to Big Flat Campground. (As of early 1981, public vehicular travel along Coffee Creek Road beyond here was not permitted. However, this management policy may change, so you might want to check at the Coffee Creek Ranger Station beforehand to learn if parking at the Ward Lake trailhead is possible.) Turn right and drive 100 feet to parking spaces. The owners of the majority of cars here most likely are hiking or backpacking to the Caribou Lakes (No. 20).

Retrace your route back up to Coffee Creek Road, turn right and after 75 feet pass the trail to the Yellow Rose and LeRoy Mines (No. 24). Continue along the road, past a locked gate, for a total of 2.3 miles from the parking area to a sign identifying the trail to Kidd Creek, Ward Lake and Swift Creek. As road walks go, this stretch is not at all irksome as it passes many clearings, viewpoints and large, lush meadows.

Turn left onto the trail and climb through woods at a gradual grade except for one short set of steep switchbacks. At an unmarked fork keep left and 0.7 mile from the road come to the signed junction of the trail to Sawtooth Ridge (No. 22). Keep left again and climb considerably more steeply along a very rocky trail. Pass a source of water and continue up near Kidd Creek. At 4.0 miles cross it at an easy ford in a clearing, a good spot for a snack stop.

Continue uphill but at a more moderate grade and along a smoother tread. Travel through less dense woods and come to a lovely, large meadow. Near the head of the valley follow the tread as it curves right and continue in the same direction you were heading as you cross a 50 foot marshy area where the route is faint. Begin winding up the complex head of the valley. You can't see the pass you'll be crossing until just before you reach it.

From the crest you'll have a good view north along the ridge top to Red Rock Mountain, Preachers Peak and Sunrise Pass (see No. 24), northwest to the Big Flat area, directly down onto Ward Lake and into the head of the Swift Creek valley. Wind steeply downhill for 0.5 mile to Ward Lake. The meadow near the northeastern tip is sprinkled with marsh marigolds during early summer. To make the side trip to Horseshoe Lake or the longer treks, continue along the east shore of Ward Lake, cross the outlet and contour in a southerly direction around the ridge.

Ward Lake

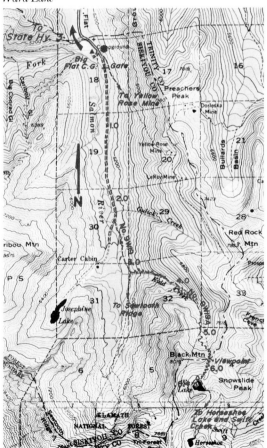

24 YELLOW ROSE and LeROY MINES

One day trip
Distance: 2.3 miles one way (to Viewpoint)
Elevation gain: 1,950 feet (to Viewpoint)
Allow 1½ hours one way
Usually open June through October
High Point: 7,000 feet (Viewpoint)
Topographic map:
   U.S.G.S. Coffee Creek, Calif.
   15'   1955

Permit Required

Most likely you'll have encountered much evidence of northwestern California's intense mining activity — past and present — long before you hike past an old digging, mine shaft or rusted remains of a boiler or stamp mill. The river beds adjacent to many roads and highways are immense rubbly ridges of tailings and today several flows — the Trinity and Salmon Rivers, for instance — support a flotilla of portable dredges. The majority of mines you pass on foot, though, were abandoned long ago.

On the scenically varied stroll up to the Yellow Rose and LeRoy Mines you'll see an assortment of remains including diggings, shafts, a boiler and even a cabin in addition to good views south and west. The meadowy area around LeRoy Mine is a delightful spot for a leisurely lunch. If you want a longer trip you can continue north, past another mine, or south for many miles.

Proceed on California 3 for 36 miles north of Weaverville or 27 miles south of Callahan to the community of Coffee Creek. Turn west and in a short distance keep straight on the Coffee Creek Road. After 4.5 miles the pavement ends and although never steep, the Cof-

fee Creek Road occasionally is narrow and rough beyond here. Pass the trailheads for hike No's. 25 through 30 and at a fork about 14 miles beyond the end of the pavement keep left and continue approximately 1.0 mile farther to the spur down to Big Flat Campground. Turn right and drive 100 feet to parking. The owners of the majority of the cars most likely are hiking or backpacking to Caribou Lakes (No. 20).

Retrace your route back up to Coffee Creek Road, turn right and after 75 feet come to a sign — that may be facing south — on the east side of the road marking the beginning of the Yellow Rose Trail. Trip No's. 22 and 23 begin farther along Coffee Creek Road. To visit the mines, though, leave the road and traverse south up along the mostly open slope, crossing several small streams. Curve into a side canyon and soon begin traveling at a more gradual grade. You can look up ahead and see debris from the Yellow Rose Mine. Pass the remains of a boiler then wind up in several short switchbacks to a weathered sign at a junction. The section to the left reaches a good viewpoint after 0.5 mile and the fork to the right passes the LeRoy Mine after 0.3 mile.

For the best views, turn left, following the arrow to Dorleska Mine and Union Lake (No. 28) and continue climbing. Curve left, traverse uphill and as you gain elevation have views southwest across the Salmon River Valley to Josephine Lake. Caribou (No. 21) and Thompson (see No. 12) Peaks to the west come into sight just before you reach a saddle at 2.3 miles near rocky outcroppings. This crest is a logical place to end this leg of the hike if you want a short outing. From here the trail descends, passing the Dorleska Mine after 0.5 mile, and continues dropping through Bullards Basin to the junction with the trail to Union Lake and other points.

To visit the more gentle setting of the LeRoy Mine, retrace your route back down to the signed junction at 1.8 miles and continue south. Cross a mostly open slope, rise moderately steeply along more woodsy terrain then round the crest of the slope and continue the final distance to the mine at a gradual grade. The stream near the building is the recommended lunch site.

The trail continues 1.5 miles southeast to Sunrise Pass and then descends into the Swift Creek valley where you can follow trails south to Horseshoe Lake (see No. 23) or east to Granite Lake (No. 31).

60

Cabin at LeRoy Mine

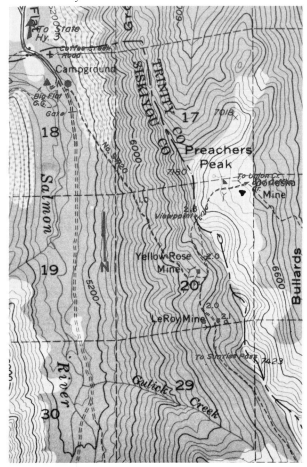

25 PACKERS PEAK

One day trip
Distance: 2.3 miles one way
Elevation gain: 2,830 feet
Allow 2½ to 3 hours one way
Usually open June through October
High Point: 7,828 feet
Topographic map:
    U.S.G.S. Coffee Creek, Calif.
    15'   1955

Permit Required

Although the 11 trails that begin from Coffee Creek Road (No's. 20 through 30) have particular scenic characteristics, the short, demanding ascent of Packers Peak is especially individualistic. None of the others travels mostly along pine and manzanita covered slopes or demands as much attention to route finding as does this climb. The lure of the hike, aside from the unique landscape and the challenge of reaching the summit, is the far-ranging view that befits the site of a former lookout. If you're the type who enjoys identifying every peak and ridge you see, carry a Forest Service recreation map for the Trinity National Forest.

Drive on California 3 for 36 miles north of Weaverville or 27 mile south of Callahan to the community of Coffee Creek. Turn west and in a short distance keep straight on Coffee Creek Road. After about 4.5 miles the pavement ends and although never steep, Coffee Creek Road occasionally is narrow and rough beyond here. Pass the trailheads for hike No's. 26 through 30 and approximately 13 miles from the end of the pavement in a big, flat, open area come to a sign identifying the start of the Packers Peak Trail.

Begin from the west side of the road and follow the faint tread along the north side of a gully and enter woods. Begin climbing gradually and just beyond where you leave the trees but before the debris from a small old mine curve sharply up and rise steeply. You can continue up the wash for water, the only source along the hike. Wind up in short switchbacks and where a trail heads right you can follow it (or another a short distance farther) and then travel through another digging.

Continue climbing and as you gain elevation travel through woods of increasingly widely spaced trees. Although no promises are made, it's on less frequented hikes such as this that you're more likely to see bear and other furtive animals. Keep on the south facing side of the slope and traverse. Where you come to a lone pine tree at a patch of manzanita continue traversing. Beyond the shrubs near 1.8 miles the tread is faint. Turn right here and climb, bearing slightly left, until you intersect the resumption of the obvious trail.

Your destination is the peak at the head of the valley. The trail generally climbs near the crest in a straight alignment. Eventually, you'll be able to see Coyote Peak just north of Packers Peak and you can turn around for a view of Billys Peak, a massive ridge whose southeast end is at the community of Coffee Creek. Mt. Shasta is visible on the northeastern horizon. Come to the remains of the lookout and continue along the summit ridge a short distance farther to a better viewpoint.

You can see south as far as Granite Peak and northwest to Preston Peak, the granite crags around Hancock Lake and beyond to the Klamath Mountains. Closer points include Caribou Mountain (see No. 21) and Sawtooth Ridge (No. 22) to the south, Thompson Peak (see No. 12) to the southwest and the Salmon River Valley below.

62

The Trinity Alps from Packers Peak

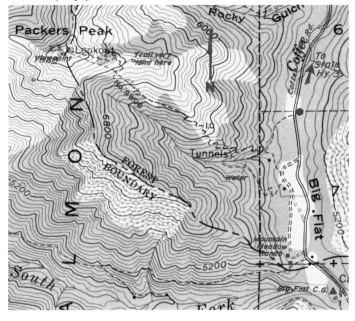

26 ADAMS LAKE

One-half day trip
Distance: 2.6 miles one way
Elevation gain: 1,300 feet; loss 150 feet
Allow 1½ hours one way
Usually open June through October
High Point: 6,200 feet
Topographic map:
  U.S.G.S. Coffee Creek, Calif.
  15   1955

Permit Required

Wildlife is abundant throughout northwestern California and on the short, but sometimes steep, climb to Adams Lake you'll have an especially good chance of seeing deer and — if you're very lucky — a young fawn or two. The hike, though certainly pleasing, is not a scenic heavyweight. This evaluation isn't necessarily a negative one since sometimes an unassuming trip is precisely what you feel like. Although the route follows a road for most of the distance, it is closed to motor vehicles and portions are fast deteriorating to a trail width, so it's not too intrusive.

Proceed on California 3 for 36 miles north of Weaverville or 27 miles south of Callahan to the community of Coffee Creek. Turn west and in a short distance keep straight on Coffee Creek Road. After 4.5 miles the pavement ends and although never steep, the road occasionally is narrow and rough beyond here. Pass the trailheads for hike No's. 27 through 30 and 11 miles beyond the end of the pavement come to a road from the right (north) shoulder whose end has been truncated. A sign just beyond it says no parking is allowed ahead. You can park east of the sign, however, and if there isn't room here two turnouts for additional cars are off the north side of Coffee Creek Road a couple of hundred feet back down to the east. Hike No's. 20 through 25 begin farther along Coffee Creek Road.

Walk up the side road, passing a sign stating it is closed to motor vehicles and then a gate. Wind up through woods along the old bed in three more turns. At 0.5 mile begin climbing more steeply along the crest of a ridge and then after 1.2 miles begin traversing down, losing about 100 feet of elevation. Travel at a gradual grade and then climb briefly before another stretch of downhill.

Come to a fork, turn right and soon begin climbing moderately near Adams Creek. Just beyond a pretty little grassy clearing have an easy ford of the outlet from Adams Lake and travel for 0.2 mile through grassy terrain sprinkled with an attractive number of rocks, boulders and trees to a camp area near the lake. The path from here to the shore is outlined with rocks.

Old saw at Adams Lake

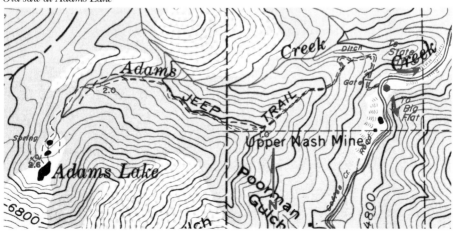

27 SOUTH FORK COFFEE CREEK TRAIL

One day trip or backpack
Distance: 5 miles one way
Elevation gain: 2,300 feet
Allow 3 hours one way
Usually open late May through October
High Point: 6,850 feet
Topographic map:
U.S.G.S. Coffee Creek, Calif.
15'   1955

Permit Required

The convoluted topography of northwestern California in concert with the inter-connecting network of trails means that hikers frequently cross or end at divides separating different watersheds. Such is the case with the trip up the valley holding the South Fork of Coffee Creek to South Fork Divide. Water from its north side eventually enters the Salmon River. From the ridge top you can see down to Trail Gulch Lake (No. 15) and you could follow a trail to it.

Drive on California 3 for 36 miles north of Weaverville or 27 miles south of Callahan to the community of Coffee Creek. Turn west and in a short distance keep straight on Coffee Creek Road. After 4.5 miles the pavement ends and although never steep, Coffee Creek Road occasionally is narrow and rough beyond here. Pass the trailheads for hike No's. 28 through 30 and 10 miles beyond the end of the pavement come to the signed beginning of the South Fork Coffee Creek Trail off the right (north) side of the road. Trip No's. 20 through 26 begin farther along Coffee Creek Road.

Walk up the road, switchback twice and where a spur goes up to the left, keep straight (right). Continue rising and then descend. At the crossing of a small stream where logs mark the location of a former bridge, look downslope for an old building. Resume climbing and cross a large stream that also probably doesn't flow all year. A bit farther cross another creek, pass a camp area near the foundation for a building and cross a wee, lush grassy clearing to the start of the trail proper. The mileages on the sign here are a bit off. Most likely the distances refer to those along an abandoned trail to Long Gulch Lake (No. 15) that you'll pass farther on.

Traverse the wooded slope above the South Fork of Coffee Creek, cross a good sized side stream and continue up at a moderate grade through a portion of the forest where ferns and grass combine in an attractive ground cover. At an unsigned fork keep right, cross the South Fork and farther on at a second, less obvious fork, to Trail Gulch Divide, keep left on the main trail. Continue up for a short distance, cross another stream and travel through more open woods to a big, somewhat scraggy clearing. As you progress up the valley the vegetation becomes more pleasingly lush.

Travel near the South Fork for awhile and then continue through clearings and open woods. As studying a map will show, calling the stream the South Fork of Coffee Creek isn't logical. Make a short, steep switchback and come to an extensive open area. As the tread becomes faint continue in the same direction you were heading, following periodic cairns. A short distance before the head of the valley look left for a trail into the woods. After 100 yards it crosses the South Fork and comes to a camp area.

However, to reach the divide, continue in the same direction you were heading and travel gradually up the valley along the open slope. Around the first part of July the ground is carpeted with star-shaped white flowers. Eventually, the trail becomes defined again. Enter woods and traverse steeply up the south slope of the valley to the signed crest. Turn right and walk up along the ridge top for a good view onto Trail Gulch Lake.

In addition to the 1.0 mile, 400 foot descent to Trail Gulch Lake, you could head west from the sign at the crest of the divide along the head of South Fork valley and beyond to Rush Creek Lake. A 1.2 mile side trip to Fish Lake (No. 14) is another possibility. Originally, the connector headed northwest from the crest but it may have been relocated down the trail to Long Gulch Lake. Lastly, the terrain comprising the South Fork valley is good for cross-country exploration.

The Upper Meadow

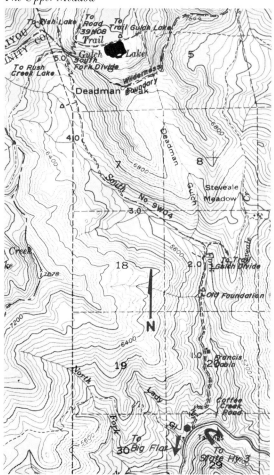

28 UNION LAKE

One day trip or backpack
Distance: 5.9 miles one way
Elevation gain: 1,750 feet
Allow 3 hours one way
Usually open June through October
High Point: 6,050 feet
Topographic map:
   U.S.G.S. Coffee Creek, Calif.
   15'   1955

Permit Required

Being labeled "typical" is no denegration when applied to a trail in the Trinity Alps. For here the adjective means the route passes through lush meadows to at least one lake and along the way trails head off through additional meritorious terrain to other destinations. Using the above definition, the hike to Union Lake is indeed typical. Also like several other trips in northwestern California, the first few miles are along an old roadbed but this man-made feature isn't aesthetically jarring as it is deteriorating rapidly. For those above noted side trips you can head west through Bullards Basin to the Dorleska Mine and beyond (see No. 24) or east to Foster Lake. More demanding is the climb and des-

cent to the trail to Sugar Pine Lake (No. 30).

Proceed on California 3 for 36 miles north of Weaverville or 27 miles south of Callahan to the community of Coffee Creek. Turn west and in a short distance keep straight on Coffee Creek Road. After 4.5 miles the pavement ends and although never steep, the road occasionally is narrow and rough beyond here. Pass the trailheads for hike No's. 29 and 30 and 6.0 miles beyond the end of the pavement come to the signed beginning of the Union Creek Trail from the left (south) side of the road. Parking is a short distance beyond the trailhead off the north side of the road. Hike No's. 20 through 27 begin farther along Coffee Creek Road.

Make two short switchbacks at the beginning then follow up along the road as it traverses the wooded slope in a more straightforward alignment. Cross a good sized stream and about 0.3 mile beyond it you can turn left from the road at a level area and walk several yards to a large pond that is a potentially good swimming hole.

Begin descending, pass a few azalea bushes whose blooms perfume the air the first part of July and come to the bridge over Union Creek. Resume traveling gradually uphill and cross Pin Creek. Walk above a stream on a rocky tread, cross the flow and continue up over the rough surface. Just after the end of the old roadbed hop a small creek at a grassy swath and a short distance farther come to a large meadowed slope that is generous with wildflowers. A camp is below the trail at the edge of the clearing. Traverse across the width of the meadow and then climb in woods to the junction of the trail to Bullards Basin and Dorleska Mine. This route continues over an open crest and descends for 2.3 miles to Coffee Creek Road at Big Flat.

Keep straight (left) and continue through woods and meadowy areas to a stream crossing at signed Union Creek Camp. Just beyond the ford come to the junction of a trail to Foster Lake. Stay right and climb moderately through less imposing woods for 0.3 mile to the Cutoff Trail to Foster Lake and Parker Divide above Sugar Pine Lake. Obviously, you can make a little loop on the return by taking the Cutoff Trail to the junction with the first trail to Foster Lake and following the latter back to the route you followed in. Again keep right and continue up through pretty woods and past lush meadows for the final 0.5 mile to the camp area above shallow Union Lake.

68

Bridge over Union Creek

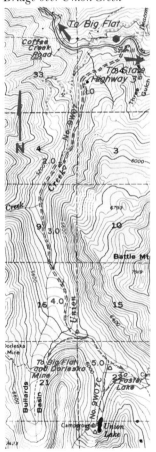

29 STODDARD LAKE

One day trip or backpack
Distance: 5 miles one way
Elevation gain: 2,350 feet
Allow 3 hours one way
Usually open June through October
High Point: 5,850 feet
Topographic map:
  U.S.G.S. Coffee Creek, Calif.
  15'   1955

Permit Required

The three special features of the hike to Stoddard Lake, the second most easterly of the 11 trails that begin from Coffee Creek Road (No's. 20 through 30), are a traverse along the wall of a deep, rocky canyon unlike any other in the area, an exceptionally good view of Billys Peak, the massive ridge whose north end looms above Stoddard Lake, and evidence, including a fascinating old wooden flume, of mining activity.

Maps indicate that a little loop is possible by heading northwest from the lake to a junction at Stoddard Meadow and then taking No. 8WO6 back to the junction at 3.9 miles. Also, as with the majority of hikes in northwestern California, you can continue considerably farther along other routes.

Drive on California 3 for 36 miles north of Weaverville or 27 miles south of Callahan to the community of Coffee Creek. Turn west and after a short distance keep straight on Coffee Creek Road. About 4.5 miles farther come to the end of the pavement and continue another 2.0 miles to a sign on the right (north) side identifying the beginning of the East Fork Coffee Creek Trail.

Wind up for a few hundred feet to a road, turn right and follow the rocky, rough bed for 0.8 mile to a sign pointing left to the trail to Stoddard and Doe Lakes. Soon switchback, traverse uphill at a moderately steep grade and then make two more short switchbacks before curving into that impressive canyon. Traverse along the rocky wall of scattered pines and manzanita. Climb steeply before and after a set of short switchbacks then resume traversing at a generally gentle grade and pass the remains of an old wooden flume.

By 1.7 miles you've hiked beyond the head of the deep lower canyon and are traveling through denser woods considerably closer to the East Fork of Coffee Creek. Pass a small stream with a pipe for obtaining water and a short distance farther come to a road. Cross a good sized stream and continue along the road, now often reduced by washouts to a narrow trail, for 0.3 mile then make two short switchbacks on a trail. Not far after the trail resumes pass a path on your right that drops to abandoned Holland Mine.

Walk briefly near the East Fork through a little meadow of grass and ferns then begin climbing and soon cross a stream. Wind up in four short switchbacks and continue climbing to a view southeast to Billys Peak.

Near 3.2 miles begin descending gradually, cross a stream then alternate between climbing and traveling on the level to another ford. Just beyond this flow come to the signed junction of the trail to Doe Lake. This route continues northeast for 0.7 mile to a fork near Stoddard Meadow then climbs west for another 2.4 miles to the small lake.

To continue the hike to Stoddard Lake, turn right, descend for 75 feet to another ford and then climb along a rocky trail. The grade moderates farther on. Pass through a grassy area a short distance before coming to a brushy section of the shore. Turn right and follow the trail along the west shore, passing a good view over the lake, to a large camp area in woods at the south end of the lake, a good place for a lunch stop if you're making a day hike.

The old flume

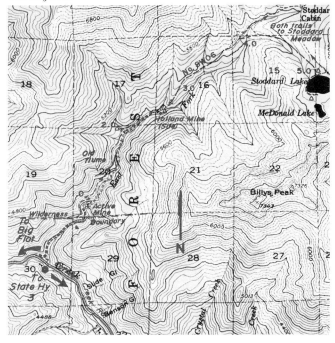

30 SUGAR PINE LAKE

One day trip or backpack
Distance: 5.4 miles one way
Elevation gain: 3,450 feet
Allow 3½ to 4½ hours one way
Usually open June through October
High Point: 6,600 feet
Topographic map:
   U.S.G.S. Coffee Creek, Calif.
   15'   1955

Permit Required

The most easterly (that is, the first after leaving California 3) of the 11 trails starting from Coffee Creek Road (No's. 20 through 30) is the route to Sugar Pine Lake that travels through several kinds of forest, ranging from scattered oaks and pines to dense stands of evergreens and across many meadows of varying sizes. Adventuresome, energetic types could continue up over Parker Divide and down through Battle Canyon to Foster and Union Lakes (No. 28) and points beyond. If you do the hike after mid-July carry water as the

tributary streams may be dry.

Proceed on California 3 for 36 miles north of Weaverville or 27 miles south of Callahan to the community of Coffee Creek. Turn west and after a short distance keep straight on Coffee Creek Road. About 4.5 miles farther come to the end of the pavement and continue another 1.0 mile to a sign pointing to Sugar Pine Trail. Turn left, drive downhill for a couple of hundred feet, cross a bridge and 60 yards farther come to the signed trailhead and turnouts for parking.

Follow the old road that heads straight to the southwest from the parking area, not the more overgrown one that curves immediately up to the right (north). Pass some madrone trees whose smooth trunks and limbs, that turn a rich, reddish-brown soon after the old bark is shed, make them easy to identify. After about 0.2 mile the road narrows into a trail that rises steadily along the wooded slope above Sugar Pine Creek. The forest cover during the first mile is a mixture of conifers and oaks and other deciduous growth but the evergreens soon become dominant and more dense.

Switchback near the 1.3 mile point and come to a stream that affords good drinking water early in the summer. As you continue climbing you frequently can see beyond the woods to the rock and bush covered ridge several hundred feet up to your right. Occasionally, the route passes through pleasing park-like settings. Just beyond 4.2 miles reach Cabin Flat and the junction of the trail to Battle Canyon and Union Lake.

Stay left, continuing in the same direction you'd been heading, and as the trail becomes faint in the deep grass at the edge of the meadow, keep straight toward the trees where the route is obvious again. Climb through woods dotted with large boulders and soon after passing the sign indicating the Wilderness boundary come to another large, grassy meadow. Keep near its west (right) edge, following cairns and blazes where the trail becomes faint. Reenter woods and continue for a short distance before crossing a meadow beneath an imposing rock ridge.

The trail follows a serpentine course through woods before crossing the rocky slope just before the lake. Good campsites are near the north shore. The brushy lake lies at the bottom of a cirque. Sugar Pine Butte rises to the southeast and the inlet creek is a waterfall that flows down the north face of the basin wall.

Sugar Pine Creek

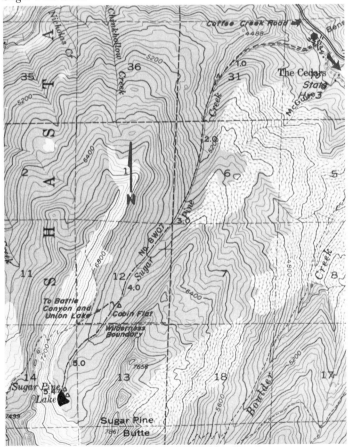

31 GRANITE LAKE

One day trip or backpack
Distance: 5.2 miles one way
Elevation gain: 2,100 feet
Allow 2½ to 3 hours one way
Usually open late June through mid-October
High Point: 6,000 feet
Topographic map:
   U.S.G.S. Trinity Lake, Calif.
   15'   1950

Permit Required

Azaleas, members of the heath family and closely related to rhododendrons, are among the most fragrant of wildflowers — only the polemoniums that grow around 13,000 feet in the Sierra come close to equaling them — and sniffing their rich, potent aroma is a frequent delight while hiking in northwestern California from mid- to late June. Their blooms are particularly plentiful along the trail to Granite Lake but the hike certainly has many other scenic charms if you're too early or late for the flower show. As is typical of most outings in the Trinities, the trail travels through forests of varying composition and across lush meadows. Another common characteristic is that you can continue by trail to other destinations, in this instance to Horseshoe Lake (see No. 23) and Deer Creek (see No. 32) that, in turn, are connected to other fine hiking areas.

Proceed about 28 miles north of Weaverville or 8.0 miles south of the community of Coffee Creek to a sign on the west side of the highway identifying the unpaved road to the Swift Creek and Lake Eleanor Trails. This junction is a short distance south of a store complex off the east side of the highway. Turn west onto the side road and after 1.0 mile keep left at a fork. Farther on the road is identified as 36N25. Four miles from the fork keep left and after 1.0 mile pass a spur on your left down to a parking area or drive 150 yards farther to the main road's end and additional parking.

Climb along the trail from the lower parking area or descend from the upper one and then follow a gentle grade. Early on pass the first of the azaleas and travel parallel to Swift Creek for 1.6 miles, crossing several small side streams that may not flow all year, to the signed junction of the Swift Creek Trail to Foster Cabin and Horseshoe Lake. As is typical of so many trails in the Trinities, the woods at the beginning of the hike are of a completely different character than those at the higher elevations of the trip.

Keep left and after several hundred feet cross the large bridge over Swift Creek. Climb and then travel at a gradual grade above Granite Creek that merges with Swift Creek just downstream from the bridge. You'll pass a few clumps of beargrass. Their tall, bulbous creamy white blooms aren't as common in northwestern California as in the Washington and northern Oregon Cascades.

Rise more steeply in a series of short windings along a sometimes rocky tread then once again hike above Granite Creek at a gentle grade. Come to a stream that's a good spot for a snack stop. If it's dry, you can rest a short distance farther at a second, larger flow that you'll come to after you begin climbing more steeply again. Cross this second creek — don't follow the path that continues straight ahead.

Continue uphill over a sometimes rocky tread then contour through an area of avalanche debris, brush, rocks and scattered trees. At the far end of the open area pass another concentration of azaleas. Travel along the edge of a meadow and then climb moderately in woods and little clearings. Wind up through a rocky area and pass a campsite in woods at the brushy end of large Gibson Meadow. Walk along its edge to an area of rocks at the south end. The little stream you parallel for a short distance is full of frogs and tiny fish. Wind up in woods for 0.2 mile and then level off just before coming to the brushy lake. For fresh water traverse west above the north shore to an inlet stream. The signed route to Deer Creek heads west over a 7,500 foot pass before dropping to a point about 0.8 mile north of Deer Lake.

Azaleas along trail

32 DEER CREEK PASS

One day trip or backpack
Distance: 7 miles one way (to Summit Lake)
Elevation gain: 4,400 feet; loss 700 feet
  (to Summit Lake)
Allow 5 to 6 hours one way (to Summit Lake)
Usually open July through October
High Point: 7,800 feet
Topographic map:
  U.S.G.S. Trinity Lake, Calif.
  15'   1950

Permit Required

During the first part of July, one of north-western California's best wildflower displays will be found in Long Canyon near the mid-point of the hike to Deer Creek Pass and Summit Lake. From the head of Long Canyon the trail traverses above lush Siligo Meadows for a mile to Deer Creek Pass that affords a bird's-eye view over Deer Lake. A trail continues another 1.5 miles to Summit Lake. Since routes also head south, west and north into fine hiking terrain this is a good backpack.

Drive on California 3 for 21 miles north of Weaverville or 7.0 miles south of Trinity Center to the signed, paved road to Long Canyon Trail. Turn west, after 3.7 miles come to a sign stating *Long Canyon Trail* a short distance beyond a marker indicating the end of the county road. Turn right onto an unpaved surface, after 0.3 mile come to a fork, keep left and go into a large parking area.

Hike steeply uphill along a road from the bulletin board. Where the bed forks keep left and eventually begin traveling along a tread that more closely resembles a trail. Cross two small streams and then at a third, larger one come to the beginning of the trail proper. Climb steeply above the East Fork of the Stuart Fork and then wind up in many short switchbacks. Pass richly fragrant azalea bushes and a few less commonly seen Washington lilies. At 1.6 miles reach the junction of the route to Bowerman Meadows.

Keep right and continue switchbacking. Soon have a view southeast to Mt. Lassen and

eventually see the head of Long Canyon. Switchback a few more times, crossing several small streams and entering the sparsely wooded terrain you'll be traveling through for the remainder of the hike. Begin traversing along the mostly open north wall of the valley through that wonderful garden of wildflowers. Cross a good sized side stream and a grassy, marshy patch before fording two adjacent flows on the valley floor and winding up the the opposite side of the canyon in about a dozen short switchbacks to a little basin on the canyon wall.

Traverse out of the bench past a stupendous display of anemonies, make two short switchbacks and curve into the valley of rocks and grass below Bee Tree Gap. Wind up to the crest and the junction of the trail to Stonewall Pass and points south.

Turn right onto the upper trail, descend briefly and where you come to a grassy swath cross it and stay on the high trail. The gentle terrain of Siligo Meadows below makes for easy cross-country exploring but since grazing is allowed in the area, don't drink from any of the streams. Climb briefly and then traverse at a gradual grade along the rocky, tree dotted basin wall to the junction of the route to the Red Mountain Trail and Stoney Creek that connects with the trail from Bee Tree Gap.

Keep right and a short distance farther come to Deer Creek Pass. You can see a section of the trail to Summit Lake winding up the west wall of the basin and north to Horse Heaven on the south end of Sawtooth Ridge (No. 22) and beyond to Caribou Mountain (see No. 21). From the pass descend for a few hundred linear feet to a junction at a lone tree. To reach Summit Lake turn left and climb to the crest where you can see your destination. Descend to a large pile of rocks in the middle of the path, turn left and follow the trail down to the northwest shore.

The route north from Deer Lake connects with trails to Sawtooth Ridge, Granite Lake (No. 31), Emerald and Sapphire Lakes (No. 33) and other scenic areas.

Bee Tree Gap

33 EMERALD and SAPPHIRE LAKES

Backpack
Distance: 14 miles one way
Elevation gain: 3,550 feet; loss 300 feet
Allow 7 to 8½ hours one way
Usually open June through October
High Point: 5,900 feet
Topographic maps:
  U.S.G.S. Cecilville, Calif.
  15'   1955
  U.S.G.S. Coffee Creek, Calif.
  15'   1955
  U.S.G.S. Helena, Calif.
  15'   1951
  U.S.G.S. Trinity Lake, Calif.
  15'   1950

Permit Required

The trip to Emerald and Sapphire Lakes up the valley of the Stuart Fork is one of the most popular in the Trinities. Among its many scenic virtues is the traverse of immense Morris Meadows. For a longer outing you can continue north to Caribou Lakes (No. 20), east into the network of trails in the Deer Creek area (see No. 32) and west over a high ridge and down the Bear Creek Trail to the trail to Canyon Creek Lakes (No. 36). A challenging 4.0 mile side trip reaches less visited Alpine Lake (No. 34).

Proceed on California 3 for 13 miles north of Weaverville or 15 miles south of Trinity Center to the signed Trinity Alps Road that begins just north of a long bridge over the reservoir inlet. Turn west and after about 1.5 miles enter a resort area. Come to the end of the pavement near some corrals, bear left, then pass more corrals and a sign identifying the way to the Stuart Fork Trail. Follow the narrow and rough, but never steep, road for 1.5 miles more and a few hundred feet beyond the entrance to Bridge Campground reach the parking area.

Walk along the road, keeping right where the bed forks, and then follow an obvious trail through a gravel area. Where the road again branches keep left, following a sign, and a short distance farther begin traveling along a trail. Cross Sunday Creek, make two short switchbacks and farther on, where the trail forks, keep right. Climb above some slippage and then descend back to the original tread. Soon begin traveling near the Stuart Fork again and traverse along the wooded slope at an erratic, but mostly moderately uphill grade. Cross signed Little Deep and then Deep Creeks. Camp areas are beyond each of the flows.

Rise away from the river a second time, pass a sign identifying Oak Flat, noteworthy for its lack of oaks, and return close to the Stuart Fork. Just beyond the sign marking the Wilderness boundary pass a camping spot just before a small stream and then reach the junction of the route to Alpine Lake and also over Canyon Creek Divide.

Keep right, pass a sign identifying Nancy Creek across the canyon and travel beside abandoned Buckeye Ditch, one of the many examples of past mining activity along the trail. Ford Salt Creek and after 0.5 mile descend to the bridge over Deer Creek. Regain the elevation you just lost and 0.5 mile farther come to signed Cold Spring Camp, a good place for a snack stop. After another 0.2 mile come to the junction of the Deer Creek Trail.

Stay left and in a short distance reach the southern edge of huge Morris Meadows, a notorious habitat for rattlesnakes so scan the trail ahead while hiking and watch where you sit or put your hands. Don't harm any you might see — only avoid them. Walk along the western side to a wooden shelter, a favored house for those snakes. Cross the meadow to its eastern side and climb gradually along grass and brush covered hillsides and through small wooded areas to a metal sign identifying Portuguese Camp, the last before Emerald Lake. One-third mile farther come to the junction of the route to the Caribou Lakes, keep left and climb along the almost treeless slope to Emerald Lake.

To reach Sapphire Lake turn right near the northeast shore and follow the trail above the lake. The route is sometimes faint as it rises among boulders above the west end of Emerald Lake but generally it's easily followed. Sapphire Lake is situated in a rocky cirque and its outlet, like that of Emerald Lake, was once dammed. There are no good campsites here.

Sapphire Lake

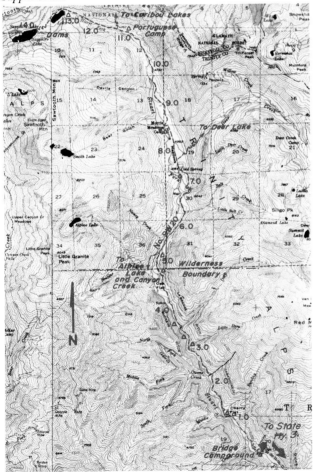

34 ALPINE LAKE

One day trip or backpack
Distance: 9 miles one way
Elevation gain: 3,600 feet
Allow 5 to 6 hours one way
Usually open late June through October
High Point: 6,100 feet
Topographic map:
U.S.G.S. Trinity Lake, Calif.
15'   1950

Permit Required

Most hikers who begin on Trail No. 9W20 intend to take it the 14 miles up the Stuart Fork valley to Emerald and Sapphire Lakes (No. 33). However, those who never follow the 4.0 spur to Alpine Lake, which leaves the main trail at the 5.1 mile point, are missing a special treat. The climb is satisfyingly demanding, often through terrain somewhat atypical of the usual Trinity Alps landscape, to an exceptionally lush meadow just below the rock wall-rimmed lake.

Carry tennis shoes for the ford of the Stuart Fork at 5.2 miles. Although normally not a problem even as early as the first part of July, you can't avoid getting your feet and legs wet. Because of this crossing, you shouldn't do the hike much earlier in the season or immediately after exceptionally heavy rains.

Drive on California 3 for 13 miles north of Weaverville or 15 miles south of Trinity Center to the signed Trinity Alps Road that begins just north of a long bridge over a reservoir inlet. Turn west and after about 1.5 miles enter a resort area. Come to the end of the pavement near some corrals, bear left past more corrals and a sign identifying the way to the Stuart Fork Trail. Follow the narrow and rough, but never steep, road for 1.5 miles

more and a few hundred feet beyond the entrance to Bridge Campground reach the parking area.

Walk along the road, keeping right where the bed forks, and then follow an obvious trail through a gravel area. Where the road again branches keep left, following a sign and a short distance farther begin traveling along a trail. Cross Sunday Creek, make two short switchbacks and farther on, where the trail forks, keep right. Climb above some slippage and then descend back to the original tread. Soon begin traveling near the Stuart Fork again and traverse along the wooded slope at an erratic, but mostly moderately uphill, grade. Cross signed Little Deep and then Deep Creeks. Camp areas are beyond each of the flows.

Travel up and away from the river a second time, pass a small sign identifying Oak Flat and return close to the river. A short distance beyond the Wilderness boundary sign pass a camping spot just before a small stream and then reach the junction of the Alpine Lake trail.

Turn left and descend to the ford of the Stuart Fork. After crossing it, continue west several yards to the base of the steep slope then turn left and traverse up along an obvious tread. After one switchback curve into the canyon holding Boulder Creek and travel through woods that are a pleasing mix of oak, pine, dogwood, rocks and, farther on, some cedar and grassy patches. At a more open area come to the junction of the trail that climbs to Canyon Creek Divide and descends the other side (No. 38) to the beginning of the popular route to Canyon Creek Lakes (No. 36).

Turn right and wind up on a trail that becomes increasingly rocky as it gains elevation. Travel along a slope of brush and scattered pines and then switchback and traverse up past dense oak bushes and scattered deer brush. Eventually, you'll be above the tall timber and have views back to the Deer Creek area (see No. 32).

Just beyond a pretty little stream bear slightly left and continue winding up over more alpine terrain. Cross the outlet of Alpine Lake and a short distance farther come near a very lush meadow. Where the trail forks keep left and traverse above the meadow and its attendant pond. Watch for where the trail recrosses the outlet, follow the level tread through grass and past trees and rocks for the remaining short distance to the lake.

Falls below the meadows

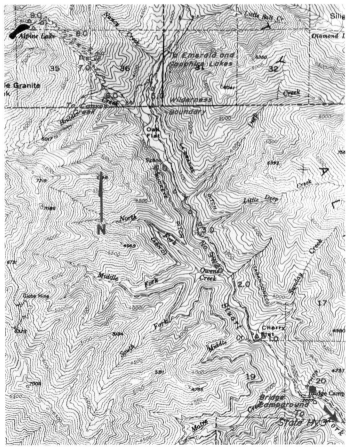

81

35 RUSH CREEK LAKES

One day trip or backpack
Distance: 7 miles one way
Elevation gain: 3,550 feet; loss 600 feet
Allow 4 to 4½ hours one way
Usually open June through October
High Point: 6,600 feet
Topographic map:
  U.S.G.S. Trinity Lake, Calif.
  15'   1950

No Permit Required

Although the trip to Rush Creek Lakes has appeal for all hikers, it will especially be enjoyed by those with more experience as the final 0.5 mile involves easy to moderately demanding cross-country travel. The vegetation is as complex as the trail alignment with the route beginning in pine and oak forests, entering dense coniferous woods as it gains elevation and then winding up open slopes of manzanita before the final stretch through lovely alpine terrain to the lake. More agile and adventuresome types can scramble up to the highest lake.

NOTE: Although the road to the trailhead is neither narrow nor steep, its reddish dirt surface become dangerously slick when wet. Carry chains if there's a chance of rain and definitely use them when the surface is wet. Fortunately, this troublesome surface isn't found on most roads to trailheads in the area.

Drive on California 3 for about 10 miles north of Weaverville or 18 miles south of Trinity Center to a sign on the west side of the highway identifying Road 34N74 to Kinney Camp and Rush Creek Lakes Trail. Turn west and after about 2.0 miles come to the junction of the spur to Kinney Camp. Keep straight (right) and continue another 2.0 miles, staying on 34N74 that is clearly identified at all junctions, to a sign identifying the beginning of the Rush Creek Lakes Trail.

Rise in traverses and switchbacks at a moderate grade to a crest, curve left then continue traversing and winding up and turn left through a thistle patch to a crest again. Note this turn as it's easy to miss on the return. Keep climbing, crossing back and forth over the ridge, and then near 2.4 miles traverse across rocky terrain scattered with low bushes and trees to a level crest where you can see south to Weaverville and west ahead to the trail winding up the brushy slope.

Turn right, after several yards resume traveling on an obvious tread and traverse down through deep woods. Curve west, following the alignment of the ridge, and traverse along its south slope at an erratic grade. Near 3.9 miles come to the edge of the tall timber and begin winding very steeply up the open slope of manzanita, oak and scattered conifers that you saw from the crest at 2.7 miles. You'll have good views north down into the valley of the Stuart Fork whose upper end holds Emerald and Sapphire Lakes (No. 33). Although you'll have occasional respites, most of the climb up the manzanita slope is at a steep grade. Canyon Creek Lakes (No. 36) are at the head the valley beyond the high, light colored ridge to the southwest.

Eventually, curve around to the west side of the slope and then begin winding downhill. Reenter woods and continue descending, periodically heading in a direction up to 180° away from your destination. Cross a stream at 6.3 miles that may not flow all year, climb briefly and where you round the nose of a low, open ridge above a little inner valley you can see ahead to the lake basin. Descend for a short distance and then begin traversing up the rocky slope. Bear slightly right where the tread is faint and farther on cross a stream. Several yards beyond it turn left at the base of a cluster of boulders and head several yards up to its top. Curve right and walk toward the basin. The tread is obscure here but the going is easy. Continue to the far end of a little grass rimmed lake, cross the inlet and work your way to the opposite (northwest) shore. Scramble up a gulley for about 75 feet and then have easy cross-country over rock slabs to the middle lake. As you climb above the grass surrounded lake you can see back (northeast) to a larger one on a rocky bench.

Monument Peak

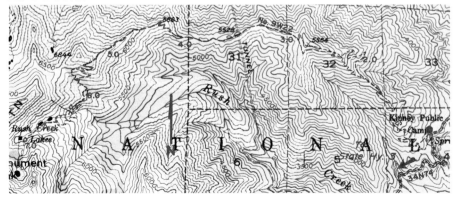

83

36 CANYON CREEK LAKES

One day trip or backpack
Distance: 8 miles one way
Elevation gain: 2,900 feet
Allow 4 to 5 hours one way
Usually open June through mid-October
High Point: 5,800 feet
Topographic map:
U.S.G.S. Helena, Calif.
15'   1951

Permit Required

The trail up deep, narrow and rugged Canyon Creek valley to the lakes at its head is one of the most heavily used in the Trinity Alps. What lures these hordes is the dramatic landscape of rock walls and pinnacles, a grandiose setting rather like the High Sierra. Because of its popularity, this is a good trip to make after Labor Day. Do not consume untreated water from Canyon Creek or any of the lakes.

Two other routes begin from the same trailhead. A 1.9 mile spur to Boulder Creek Lakes (No. 37) leaves the main trail at 6.7 miles but the short distance belies the difficulty of the hike. The second, the Bear Creek Trail (No. 38), climbs to the crest of the high divide that forms the east wall of Canyon Creek valley.

Drive west of Weaverville on California 299 for 8.0 miles to Junction City and at its east end turn north onto signed Canyon Creek Road. After 10 miles keep right at a fork — don't take the road up to the left. About 1.5 miles farther pass the signed entrance to Ripstein Campground, after less than a mile come to the end of the pavement and continue the final short distance to the parking loop.

Walk to the upper (northeast) end of the parking area, keep left, as indicated by a sign, and travel on the level for 0.3 mile to the crossing of Bear Creek, the last source of water for 3.0 miles. Begin climbing gradually

along the oak covered lower slopes of the canyon wall. Near 2.7 miles make one set of switchbacks and soon come to a grassy clearing that affords a good view of the granite pinnacles on the west wall. Several hundred feet farther pass a sign pointing left to McKay Camp.

Begin climbing more noticeably and come to an area of granite blocks. Cross a stream, the first source of water since Bear Creek, and then make two switchbacks, recrossing the flow after each turn. The canyon broadens and you'll have a good view north up to Sawtooth Mountain and across the canyon to Lower Canyon Creek Falls, the largest cascade in the drainage. Come to a crest above a more modest sized waterfall then walk through the gorgeous setting of lush Upper Canyon Creek Meadows where the flow of Canyon Creek is quiet for the first time. Pass a large camp area on your right formed by a huge overhanging boulder, obviously a good spot when the weather is foul.

Continue generally along Canyon Creek, veering away periodically and passing many good campsites. Along one stretch travel through a grove of exceptionally tall Douglas fir and cedar. Come to a signed side path that goes left (west) for 100 yards to a view of Middle Falls. Climb in short switchbacks, passing a water source on your right, to the signed junction of the trail to Boulder Creek Lakes.

Stay right and travel near Canyon Creek again, cross a small side stream and wind up in many switchbacks, leaving the woods, to a view of Upper Falls. Come to a small bench and another section of quiet water. A side path here heads left to a camp area. To reach Stone House, another overhanging boulder, continue west, ford Canyon Creek and walk into the woods.

To complete the hike, wind up along open slopes on the rough, rocky trail to the outlet from the lower lake and the end of the official trail. Turn left onto a use-path, ford the stream and come to the lower lake where the rule about camping at least 200 feet from shore is waived as there aren't any sites beyond this minimum.

To reach the upper, larger lake follow the use-trail along the south side of the lower lake and continue up in the same general direction you were heading for 300 yards. For more solitude and/or superb scenery you can head northeast for 1.4 miles cross-country up to "L" Lake.

Lower Canyon Creek Lake (above) Portion of trail (below)

37 BOULDER CREEK LAKES

One day trip or backpack
Distance: 8.6 miles one way
Elevation gain: 2,900 feet; loss 150 feet
Allow 5 to 6 hours one way
Usually open late June through mid-October
High Point: 5,750 feet
Topographic map:
  U.S.G.S. Helena, Calif.
  15'   1951

Permit Required

The final mile to Boulder Creek Lakes is, foot for foot, the most demanding in this guide. If you'll be carrying a heavy pack, include a rope for use in lowering it down the few rock pitches. The first 6.7 miles follows the magnificently scenic but heavily used trail to Canyon Creek Lakes (No. 36). Do not consume untreated water from Canyon Creek or from the lakes.

Proceed west of Weaverville on California 299 for 8.0 miles to Junction City and at its east end turn north onto signed Canyon Creek Road. After 10 miles keep right at a fork, continuing on the paved road — don't take the route up to the left. About 1.5 miles farther pass the signed entrance to Ripstein Campground, after less than a mile come to the end of the pavement and continue the final short distance to the parking loop.

Begin from the upper end of the parking area where a sign also marks the Bear Creek Trail (No. 38), keep left and travel on the level for 0.3 mile to the crossing of Bear Creek, the last source of water for 3.0 miles. Begin climbing gradually beneath oak and near 2.8 miles come to a grassy clearing that affords a good view of granite pinnacles on the west wall. Several hundred feet farther pass McKay Camp.

Begin climbing more noticeably and come to an area of granite blocks. Cross a stream and then make two switchbacks, refording the flow after each turn. The canyon broadens and you'll have a good view north up to Sawtooth Mountain and across the canyon to Lower Canyon Creek Falls, the largest cascade in the drainage. Come to a crest above a more modest sized waterfall then walk through the gorgeous setting of lush Upper Canyon Creek Meadows where the flow of Canyon Creek is quiet for the first time. Pass a camp area on your right formed by a huge overhanging boulder.

Continue generally along Canyon Creek past many good campsites and along one stretch travel through a grove of exceptionally tall Douglas fir and cedar. Come to a signed side path that goes left (west) for 100 yards to a view of Middle Falls. Climb in short switchbacks, passing a water source on your right, to the signed junction of the Boulder Creek Lakes trail.

Turn left and descend in two short switchbacks. Just before Canyon Creek veer right onto a side path and head about 50 yards upstream to a possible large log across the flow. From the campsite on the opposite side turn left and walk back to the main trail. Wind up the manzanita and granite boulder dotted slope past a grove of small aspen. The trail stops at the edge of a meadow but it resumes at 2 o'clock on the opposite side of the small clearing.

Continue up, alternating between meadows and clumps of woods, to near the base of a cliff band of black rock. Here the trail gradually curves right and begins an incredibly steep climb along a rocky tread that doesn't provide good footing. At the top of this pitch turn left (south) and follow cairns in a curve to the right around a huge granite mound and come to the edge of a 100 foot deep rectangular chasm.

Descend this cliff face directly below the last cairn. Do not attempt to cross on the seemingly easier slopes upstream as the gorge becomes even more steep and dangerous. Pick your way down to the short section of trail at the base of the cliff and cross two forks of Boulder Creek to the opposite wall. The best route is just to the right of the waterfall and directly up. The pitch to the left is very steep and of even looser rock. From the top of the cliff head 50 yards south to several good campsites near the north shore of the lower lake.

Boulder Creek Lake

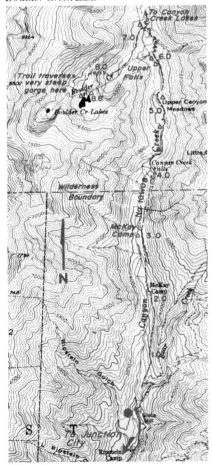

38 BEAR CREEK TRAIL

One day trip
Distance: 4.7 miles one way
Elevation gain: 3,360 feet
Allow 3 to 3½ hours one way
Usually open late May through October
High Point: 6,360 feet
Topographic maps:
  U.S.G.S. Helena, Calif.
  15'   1951
  U.S.G.S. Trinity Lake, Calif.
  15'   1950

No Permit Required

The Bear Creek Trail, which doesn't follow but instead only fords several forks of its namesake once each, is an interesting complement to the two other routes (No's. 36 and 37) that begin from the same parking area. The last two travel up the floor of impressive Canyon Creek valley in contrast to the Bear Creek Trail that climbs in a circuitous route through several vegetation zones to a rocky ridge that forms the divide between the Stuart Fork and Canyon Creek drainages. The odds are relatively high that you'll see, or at least hear, a rattlesnake or two along the hike, so continually scan the trail ahead and always check the area before you sit down or get drinking water. Don't molest the snakes.

Drive west of Weaverville on California 299 for 8.0 miles to Junction City and at its east end turn north onto signed Canyon Creek Road. After 10 miles keep right at a fork, continuing on a paved road — don't take the route up to the left. About 1.5 miles farther pass the signed entrance to Ripstein Campground, after less than a mile come to the end of the pavement and continue the final short distance to the parking loop.

Walk to the upper (northeast) end of the parking area to a sign, keep straight (right) and wind up the road in five switchbacks beneath a forest of oak, maple, dogwood and conifers. Cross a small stream that probably dries up later in the summer and begin walking along a narrower bed. Traverse to a good sized creek and beyond it abruptly begin traveling through a less lush cover of pine and manzanita.

Travel in and out of a small side canyon with a little stream and begin winding up in several loose switchbacks. Climb steeply as you leave a section of woods then begin a long, level traverse, during which the road becomes a trail. Where a faint path heads uphill to the Globe Mill continue straight and on the level. Along the traverse and for the remainder of the hike you'll have extensive views, particularly of the massive ridge above.

Curve into the deep side canyon that holds the forks of Bear Creek and ford two branches of the flow. Tiger lilies and other large wildflowers bloom here the first part of July. Continue on the level to a third flow, immediately beyond it resume climbing and wind up in six switchbacks through a grove of tall pines and other conifers to the crest of a northeast-southwest oriented ridge and the faint junction of an abandoned trail to the valley floor. Traverse uphill, leaving the crest, in attractive woods of large trees and lush undergrowth.

Come to a side stream and a few hundred feet farther a second one, the last source of water. After traversing a short distance farther begin climbing directly up the face of the ridge. Shift into compound low and wind up very steeply along the brush covered slope for 0.7 mile to the crest of the divide. Turn right and after 50 feet pass the continuation of the trail that winds down the other side and connects with the trails to Alpine Lake (No. 34) and farther down the route to Emerald and Sapphire Lakes (No. 33). The middle section of this route may be faint and you'll need a wilderness permit to visit these areas. For more extensive views, continue southeast along the crest and have an easy scramble to a rocky perch.

Tiger Lilies

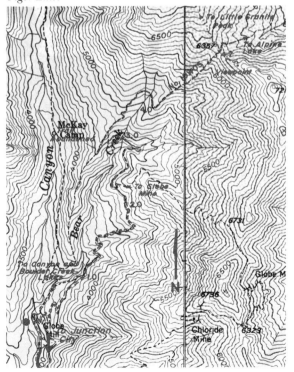

39 BLACK BUTTE

One day trip
Distance: 2.5 miles one way
Elevation gain: 1,835 feet
Allow 1½ to 2 hours one way
Usually open June through October
High Point: 6,325 feet
Topographic map:
   U.S.G.S. Weed, Calif.
   15'   1954

No Permit Required

The symmetrical shape of Black Butte just west of the considerably more irregular and massive bulk of Mt. Shasta is an obvious landmark to motorists on I-5. A fire lookout that once perched on the summit was removed in the fall of 1975 but the panorama from the three pronged pinnacle is unchanged: Mt. Shasta (see No. 40) with Shastina on its western flank fill the space to the northeast, the spire of Mt. McLoughlin in Oregon juts up from the northern horizon, Mt. Eddy (see No. 18) looms across the broad valley to the west and the view south extends beyond the Castle Crags (No. 41).

The trail to the top of Black Butte is very rocky so you will be more comfortable wearing sturdy boots. Carry water as none is available along the route.

Drive on I-5 about 1.0 mile south of Weed or 6.0 miles north of Mt. Shasta City to the South Weed Boulevard exit. From the north, turn left at the end of the exit, go under the freeway and continue east for 600 feet to a T-junction and a stop sign. From the south turn right at the end of the exit and go to the stop sign. Turn right and after 0.5 mile come to the junction of a road on your left. A sign off the right shoulder of the main road points to Black Butte Lookout 7. Turn left onto a gravel surface, go 0.6 mile and curve left just before reaching the raised railroad tracks. One-tenth mile beyond the curve and across from a wreckage and salvage business take the road that heads up to a railroad crossing. Several yards east of the tracks come to a junction and turn right. After 0.3 mile keep left where a spur drops back to the tracks, go 0.1 mile farther and curve left where another road continues straight and up. Seventy-five yards farther keep left at a side loop and travel 3.0 miles to a four-way junction. Turn sharply right and go 0.4 mile to a small horse unloading ramp on your right and several turnouts. Parking spaces are not available beyond here.

You also can reach the trailhead by taking the Everitt Memorial Highway and unpaved roads from Mt. Shasta City. Acquire a sketch map of driving directions from the U.S. Forest Service office at 204 Alma in Mt. Shasta City.

From the parking turnouts, walk up the road for 0.3 mile to its end at a small turnaround where the possibly unmarked trail begins. For the entire hike the grade is moderate and steady. Traverse along the north side of the butte, soon leaving the woods. During late May and early June the rocky slope is brightened by the blooms of dogwood, penstemon, fragrant tobacco brush and other wildflowers.

Near 1.2 miles curve south and traverse along the west side for 0.2 mile. At that point turn sharply left and travel above a cleft. Curve slightly to the southeast for 0.3 mile along a steep slope then switchback three times on the north facing side. Traverse the southeast side of a second, higher rocky cleft then wind up in eight short switchbacks to the summit area. Interestingly, suggestions have been made to rename this dramatic peak Muir Butte after the famous naturalist-author John Muir, who is generally associated with the Yosemite and High Sierra regions.

Black Butte

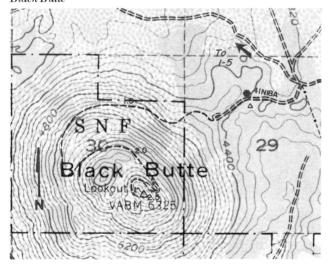

91

40 HORSE CAMP

One-half day trip or backpack
Distance: 1.6 miles one way
Elevation gain: 800 feet
Allow 1 hour one way
Usually open late June through October
High Point: 7,900 feet
Topographic map:
  U.S.G.S. Shasta, Calif.
  15'   1954

No Permit Required

Horse Camp, at timberline on Mt. Shasta's southwestern flank, is the usual beginning point for those attempting to climb the 14,162 foot peak. Although the standard routes on Mt. Shasta generally present no technical problems, crampons, ice axes, warmer clothing and the other gear and the skill peculiar to mountaineering are needed, so mere hikers shouldn't even consider trying to reach the summit. However, a good trail does head up from Horse Camp and if you want a longer hike you can follow it for some distance before coming to that line that separates safe hiking from climbing terrain. Also, the area around Horse Camp makes for attractive and interesting cross-country travel.

Leave I-5 on the Mt. Shasta City exit and near the center of town turn east on E. Alma Street, following the sign to Sand Flat. After about 0.5 mile turn left onto Everitt Memorial Highway, as indicated by the sign identifying it as the route to the Mt. Shasta Ski Bowl. Follow this road for 9.0 miles to a sign on your left listing mileages to Sand Flat and Horse Camp Trail. Turn left here onto the unpaved road. After 1.0 mile at Sand Flat keep left, as indicated by a sign pointing to Horse Camp, a short distance farther keep left again at an unsigned fork and then wind through the forest for 0.4 mile to the signed trailhead.

Hike up through a lovely park-like woods of widely spaced conifers and little ground cover and eventually begin rising at a slightly more noticeable grade. As you've already observed on the drive to the trailhead, at around the 6,000 foot level impressive forests replace the scrubby vegetation of the valley and lower slopes.

Come to the old road from Bunny Flat, veer left and continue up through more open woods that were selectively logged years ago. Walk at a more gradual grade, reenter uncut woods and stay left where a trail joins from the downslope side. Continue traversing uphill, still through most pleasing terrain, then veer north at a more gradual grade to a stone cabin. Ample water is available from a spout near the northeast side of the structure.

The building and the land surrounding it belong to the Sierra Club. You're welcome to visit the lodge but you're asked to cook and sleep outside.

To travel a ways up the mountain, continue north and east from the cabin along the obvious trail. Don't climb beyond where the tread is well-defined or make any of the possible cross-country trips if the visibility is poor. This is one of those areas where it's especially easy to become disoriented in foggy weather.

Although Mt. Whitney and a few other peaks in the Sierra are higher than Mt. Shasta by a few hundred or so feet, nothing else in California can compare with the latter's monolithic bulk. Shasta and Mt. Lassen are the most obvious features at the southern end of the volcanic range extending north through Oregon and Washington and into Canada. Shasta Indians may have called it *Wy-e-kah* and the peak was identified as Mount Jackson on early maps.

There are those who want to log the stand of virgin Shasta red firs in the area, the last on the south side of the mountains and to build a ski lift within 200 feet of Horse Camp. If you are concerned about these threats and want more information write to the Mt. Shasta Resource Council, Box 829, Mt. Shasta, California 96067.

Sierra Club Hut

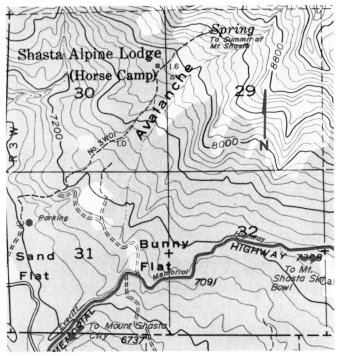

41 CASTLE DOME

One day trip
Distance: 2.7 miles one way
Elevation gain: 1,460 feet
Allow 2 hours one way
Usually open late April through early November
High Point: 4,600 feet
Topographic map:
  U.S.G.S. Dunsmuir, Calif.
  15'   1954

No Permit Required

The ridge of spires looming above I-5 just south of Dunsmuir is unique in form alone but the Castle Crags, as the outcropping is aptly named, is composed of granite, a rock not all that common in northwestern California. Certainly there are examples scattered about, such as the Little Matterhorn at the end of the Coffee Creek Road or upper Canyon Creek valley (No. 36), also in the Trinity Alps, but none in the configuration of the Castle Crags. Several trails penetrate the area and one of the best is to the base of Castle Dome. In addition to a close look at the Crags

and the hike through varied and interesting terrain, you'll have a good view of Mt. Shasta. Carry water as the only creek is off the main trail.

Proceed on I-5 to the Castella and Castle Crags State Park exit. If you're approaching from the north this exit is 6.5 miles south of Dunsmuir. Turn right at the end of the exit and follow signs to the park entrance. The day use fee is $2 and overnight camping in the park is $5. Be sure to obtain one of the little brochures that describes the geology, plant-life, human history and other trails in the area. Beyond the entrance station keep right and after 0.3 mile turn left, following the signs to Vista Point and Crags Trail. Drive through the campground and then climb steeply on a narrow road that isn't suitable for trailers for 0.6 mile to the parking area.

Walk 100 yards back from the end of the road to the sign marking the beginning of the Crags Trail and listing mileages to Castle Dome, Indian Springs and Root Creek. Travel at a gradual grade through woods for 0.3 mile to the junction of the Root Creek Trail. Keep left and switchback to a crest. Go under small power lines and where you bisect the Pacific Crest Trail No. 2000 continue in the same direction you were heading.

Continue up through a wonderfully mixed woods of incense cedar, Douglas fir, pine, maple and dogwood. The last two of course add much color to the hike during autumn. At the junction of a trail down to park head-quarters stay right and keep climbing at a moderate grade. Come to a view across to the Crags and traverse northwest and north at a gradual grade to the junction of the 0.2 mile spur to Indian Springs. The trail descends slightly to the springs and no camping is allowed there.

To continue the climb to the base of Castle Dome, keep straight (right) and beyond here the formerly smooth trail becomes rough. Soon have a view of Castle Dome and across the valley to snow covered Mt. Shasta and its subsidiary cone Shastina.

The terrain becomes rocky with manzanita bushes forming the primary ground cover between the scattered conifers. Pay attention to the alignment of the trail along this final portion so you'll have no trouble staying on the correct route on the return trip. Wind up past many interesting formations, cross another area of dense manzanita and abruptly come to the end of the trail at the base of Castle Dome.

The Castle Crags

alphabetical listing of trails

Cover Photo: Gibson Meadow below Granite Lake